# THE PARTITION AND COLONIZATION OF AFRICA

# THE
# PARTITION
## &
# COLONIZATION
## OF
# AFRICA

BY

SIR CHARLES LUCAS

HOWARD FERTIG

NEW YORK · 1972

First published in 1922


HOWARD FERTIG, INC. EDITION 1972
Published by arrangement with Oxford University Press

Library of Congress Cataloging in Publication Data

Lucas, Sir Charles Prestwood, 1853–1931.
  The partition & colonization of Africa.

  Reprint of the 1922 ed.
  Includes bibliographical references.
  1. Africa—Colonization. 2. Africa—History—1884–1950. I. Title.
DT31.L8 1972    960′.2    77–80568


PRINTED IN THE UNITED STATES OF AMERICA
BY NOBLE OFFSET PRINTERS, INC.

# PREFACE

THESE lectures were given in the first quarter of 1921, at the Royal Colonial Institute, to a study circle of teachers of the London County Council. They do not pretend to cover the whole ground but are designedly somewhat discursive, with the intention of suggesting diverse points of view and a variety of subjects for further study in one direction or another. For the same reason a good many books and papers of different kinds are quoted or referred to. While the lectures have been awaiting publication various developments have taken place in Africa, but it has not been attempted to keep pace with changes which are still in complete by alteration of the text. I am much indebted to Mr. W. S. Tomkinson for very ample revision and correction.

C. P. LUCAS.

*June,* 1922.

# CONTENTS

PAGE

I. Africa : General : in Ancient Times :
the Mediterranean World . . 9

II. Africa from Ancient Times to the
Nineteenth Century : The Natives
of Africa . . . . . 25

III. The Slave Trade : Sierra Leone and
Liberia . . . . . . 42

IV. Missionaries and Explorers : David
Livingstone . . . . . 60

V. The Scramble for Africa, 1884-91 :
the Belgian Congo : the entry of
Germany : Chartered Companies. 77

VI. The Scramble for Africa, 1891-1914 :
Railways . . . . . 100

VII. North Africa . . . . . 117

VIII. South Africa . . . . . 134

IX. West and East Africa . . . 150

X. The late Campaigns in Africa . . 176

XI. The Result of the War on the Map
of Africa : African Problems 193

# CONTENTS

PAGE

Appendix I. The Tenures of the Empire . 209

,,  II. The Meaning of Protectorate 211

,,  III. Capitulations and Extra-territorial Privileges . . . 213

,,  IV. Mandates . . . . 216

,,  V. Note on Books . . . 217

Index . . . . . . . . 219

# I

## AFRICA: GENERAL: IN ANCIENT TIMES: THE MEDITERRANEAN WORLD

THOSE who set out to teach the Geography and History of Africa should remember as the cardinal point of their teaching, that Africa, until the middle of the nineteenth century, was not thought of as a continent at all. Before then it was known to Europeans as a series of coast-lines, and even that limited knowledge was only reached in modern history. Egypt is emphatically the land of the Lower Nile, brigaded from all time with Asia more than with Africa. The north coast of Africa in old times was, and to a lesser degree still is, connected with Europe rather than with Africa; it was not so much the north of Africa as the south shore of the Mediterranean. The western side of Africa, unknown in the greater part of its length until the time which also saw the discovery of America, was connected with America more than with Africa. It was the eastern shore of the Atlantic, across which slave labour was carried to America. It was known as the West Coast of Africa, or simply the West Coast, rather than as West Africa. Similarly, the eastern side of Africa was the western shore of the Indian Ocean. It became an Arab and Asiatic, more than an African, coast. Finally, the southern end of Africa was first a stopping-point on the way to and from the East and, after the discovery of Australia, an outpost towards the South. For the white man's purpose the rim of Africa alone existed, and the rim looked outwards, not inwards. To show what Africa really was a

*Africa— never a continent till late in the nineteenth century.*

hundred years ago, we do not want maps of an immense peninsular continent, girt by the various oceans and seas, so much as maps of oceans and seas fringed by African coasts.

All this was changed after the age of Livingstone, when the great lakes were discovered and the courses of the rivers determined. Set a map of Africa, as late as 1840, by a map of fifty years later, and the eye sees at once that a continent has come into being. Instead of being arrested at coast-lines, enclosing, in the southern half of Africa, a more or less blank space, it is carried on continuously along the waterways of the interior.

*Africa the dark continent*   Africa then was the Dark Continent, because it was unknown as a continent until long after the other continents. Even Australia is hardly an exception to this fact. Stuart crossed the Australian desert from south to north in 1862, eleven years before Livingstone died. The trans-continental telegraph was carried from south to north in 1872, a year before he died. Forrest crossed the Australian desert from west to east in 1874, the year after Livingstone died. In a word Africa did not exist as one whole until quite recent times, and yet one corner of Africa, Egypt, had been known through all the centuries as a cradle of civilization.

*and therefore pre-eminently the dependent continent.*   The result of Africa being the dark continent is that, at the present day, it is the most dependent of all the continents. It is almost entirely in the stage from which other continents have emerged or, as a result of the war, are emerging with increased rapidity. The war has left Africa, in the main, as it found it, a dependency of Europe. There is only one state in Africa which really stands on its own bottom. That is our own self-governing dominion, the Union of South Africa. There are only two nominally independent states at this moment[1] in Africa. One is Abyssinia, whose independence was in 1906 jointly guaranteed by France, Italy and Great Britain. The other is the Republic of Liberia, of which more will be said hereafter, and which owes its independence, as it owed its origin, to the good offices of the United States.

Why did Africa, linked, as it is, to Asia, and at the doors of Europe, remain for so long the dark continent ? *Why was Africa the* Why was its coast-line not known earlier, and why was *dark con-* its interior largely unknown until within the lifetime of *tinent ?* elderly men and women ?  Possibly the coast-line remained unknown because the line of expanding civilized life was an east and west line, more than a north and south line ; and though the extreme breadth of Africa east and west is not far short of the extreme length north and south (very roughly 4,600 miles against 5,000), the continent clearly runs north and south more than east and west.  Outside the Mediterranean, the Red Sea coast, which was well known, was the only part of Africa which lay on the way to somewhere else. It was only when the Red Sea route was more or less blocked to Western Europe, that the coast-line of Africa was, as a result of successful endeavour to find a way round to the East, finally made known to the world.  It is not a matter for wonder that the coasts of the far south of Africa remained unexplored till the days of modern history.  The coasts of farthest Asia, at any rate north of China, were probably no better known.  It was a question of distance.  When ships were weak and resources limited, voyages were directed to some definite known point.  New worlds were brought to light not so much by attempts to find new countries as by attempts to reach old countries by new routes.

[1] January 1921.

Now comes the second and more interesting question. Why was the interior of Africa unknown for such an interminable time? The answer requires a study of the map. Africa is a huge, very compact mass of land, with an area of eleven-and-a-quarter as against barely three million square miles in Australia, which has some points in common with Africa. As a whole, Africa, which, south of the Sahara, is an elevated plateau girt by a low-lying coast-belt, is the most inaccessible of all the continents. It is also the most tropical of all the continents, and heat, just as much as cold, determines accessibility. What other conditions, apart from the kind of human inhabitants, make a land accessible? They are three in number: (1) an indented coast and 'jumping-off' places on or near the coast, (2) absence of natural barriers between the coast and the interior, and presence of natural means of communication, principally waterways, (3) a comparatively healthy climate. In all these conditions Africa is found unsatisfactory, and most unsatisfactory on the side to which penetration from Western Europe would naturally be directed, the western side. This west coast would obviously be the side on which the non-Mediterranean peoples of Western Europe, the Dutch, the Danes, the British, would make their first attempts, just as the north coast would be the natural objective for the Mediterranean peoples. Let us in the first place look at the north coast, and then at the other extreme, the southern end of Africa. On either coast the climate was not unfavourable to intruders from Europe. The north coast is sub-tropical but quite suitable for Mediterranean peoples, as is shown by French colonization in Algeria. The southern end is warm, but in the temperate zone. But the north coast so far as the Libyan desert, which makes the western frontier of Egypt, is practically an

*The inaccessibility of Africa.*

island, or a series of islands, cut off from the rest of Africa by desert as effectually as it is from Europe by sea, and in the north-west there is the further barrier of the Atlas range. Moreover, apart from geography, when modern history opened, and modern Europe began to intrude into other continents, a human element (militant Mohammedanism) was a bar to penetration into Africa from the north. In the far south, apart from its great distance from Europe, the interior can only be reached from the sea by surmounting successive heights of land. On the eastern side of the southern peninsula, the heights of land become lofty mountains; on the western side, the plateau of the interior, when reached, is desert.

West Africa is clearly the side of the continent most easily approached from Europe, but it has few 'jumping-off' places, that is, islands near the mainland and at points where it can easily be penetrated.[1] There is no group, for example, answering to the West Indies in their relation to America. Of the northern islands, the Canaries are nearest the mainland, but landing from the Canaries would mean landing on the desert. Perhaps the island of Fernando Po, off the Cameroons, best anwers to a 'jumping-off' place, and much higher up the western coast the little islands of Arguin and Goree served more or less as footholds. But, taking the whole length of this western side, it is wanting in island bases near the mainland, and the mainland is wanting in harbours. North of the Equator, the best harbour or road-

[1] It is suggested that teachers on the British Empire should emphasize the attraction of 'jumping-off' places, actual or potential, for the sea-going English race, beginning with the original landing of our English ancestors on the island of Thanet. The Far East, for example, provides abundant illustrations in Penang, Singapore, Labuan, Hong Kong, Wei-hai-wei.

stead is Sierra Leone. The Cameroon Estuary, with
Duala upon it, now in French hands, is in some ways
a good harbour, and much more landlocked than
Sierra Leone. In Portuguese Angola there are good
natural harbours, including Lobito Bay, the terminus of
the Benguela railway. Farther south is Walfish Bay,
and farther south again, nearly sixty miles short of Table
Bay, is Saldanha Bay, a really good natural harbour, but
remote, and therefore little used. There are other harbours no doubt, but the western coast-line, taken as a
whole, is badly off for harbours. The Gold Coast, for
instance, which specially attracted Europeans, has no
natural harbour. The rivers again on this western side,
as indeed on all sides of Africa, are, or were, till modern
engineering came to the rescue, very unhelpful. No
continent has rivers so bad, in proportion to their size,
for navigation. The best West African waterway, for
240 or 250 miles from the sea, is the Gambia. The
Niger, like the Zambesi on the opposite side, disperses
itself in a delta with bars and swamps, the Forcados
mouth being the best opening. Inside the delta the
Niger is better for navigation by light craft than most
African rivers, for there is no break in the river for
a long distance inland. On the Congo large vessels
cannot go up 100 miles from the sea. The southernmost of the large rivers on the western side, the Orange
river, is the most useless of all. Its mouth is barred,
and its course is in a deep channel with falls and rapids.
Suppose that this river, which flows from the centre of
the particular part of Africa which is most suited for
European colonization, and comes out on the side most
convenient for Europe, instead of tumbling down
in a deep bed from the plateau to the ocean, had been
a miniature St. Lawrence, what a help it would have

been to South Africa. And lastly, the climate of the West Coast of Africa is by repute one of the worst in the world for white men.[1]

The East Coast of Africa is far removed from Europe, and could only be reached from the Mediterranean with the goodwill of the rulers of Egypt. In the south, Table Bay is a somewhat exposed harbour. Simon's Bay is safer. Beyond the Cape, the first really fine natural harbour is Delagoa Bay, which belongs to Portugal. From this point onward, on the Central East African coast, there are quite a number of good harbours. In Portuguese territory, Beira, the outlet of Southern Rhodesia, is far from first rate, but farther north, Port Amelia, on Pemba Bay, is said to be a magnificent natural harbour. In what was German East Africa there are several harbours, such as Mikindani, Lindi, Kilwa Kisiwani, Dâr-es-Salaam and Tanga; Tanga under the Germans had by far the largest export trade. Zanzibar has a very busy harbour or roadstead, and Mombasa has two harbours, one of which, the Kilindini harbour, has been rated as the best in East Africa, though Dâr-es-Salaam is said to be superior in natural advantages. North of Mombasa, in British territory, there are one or two not first-rate harbours, and then the coast tends to become harbourless. Zanzibar and Mombasa are excellent examples of natural jumping-off places, so in a less degree are the islands of Mozambique and Kilwa, and in general the eastern side

[1] A great authority, however, Sir Hugh Clifford, now Governor of Nigeria, defends the present-day climate of West Africa. Few men have had such wide experience of tropical climates in east and west, in Malaya, Borneo, Ceylon, the West Indies, the Gold Coast, and Nigeria, and his judgement as given in his *Address to the Nigerian Council* of 29th December 1920, pp. 76-8, is that he had found the West African climate 'as tropical climates go, among the very best that I had so far sampled'.

of Africa is much more accessible than the western. The rivers, however, like other African rivers, are very poor waterways. The greatest, the Zambesi, has a delta and bars at the mouths, the best entrance being the Chinde channel, which was only discovered in 1889, by an Englishman. Inside the delta the river is shallow in the dry season, 400 miles up the navigation is entirely broken by rapids, and higher up again by the Victoria Falls. The chief river of the Tanganyika Province, late German East Africa, is the Rufiji, which again ends in a delta and is of no great use for navigation, and the Tana and Juba in British East Africa are poor waterways. Further, though the climate on the eastern side has not had so bad a reputation as that of West Africa, it is in parts very malarial, as was sufficiently proved in the campaign in German East Africa. Lastly, if we look back to Egypt, the Nile has always been used as a source of irrigation, much more than as a waterway. Indeed, it is an indifferent waterway. In High Nile there may have been in the past more or less continuous navigation, but in time of Low Nile, the cataracts were and are obstacles. Moreover, until the far interior is reached, the Nile is an isolated river, as Egypt is an isolated country, a river valley shut in by desert. Egypt has been called the narrowest country in the world; and if the immense length of the Nile, its defects as a waterway, and the fact that for so many hundreds of miles it is the one solitary avenue of advance, if these facts are remembered, it becomes plain that the continent of Africa could hardly be explored by following up the Nile.

Geography, then, adequately accounts for the immense time which elapsed before the interior of Africa was known. But human agency has been a contributory cause. The slave-trade undoubtedly helped to isolate Africa; conversely, the crusade against the slave-trade opened it up. In the north and east the antagonism of Mohammedanism to Christianity also maintained a barrier against Europe.

What did the ancients know of Africa? There is the *The Ancients' knowledge of Africa.* very familiar story, told by Herodotus, of Phoenicians sent down the Red Sea by a king of Egypt, six centuries B.C., who coasted along, landing, sowing, and reaping crops for two years, finding as they went that they had the sun on their right hand, that is in the north, a proof that they had crossed the Equator, and eventually, in the third year, returning home through the Straits of Gibraltar. There is the undoubted historic fact that some four and a half or five centuries B.C. the Carthaginians planted trading stations or colonies on the Atlantic coast of Morocco. They seem to have gone as far south as Sierra Leone and possibly traded with the Gold Coast. It has always been held that aggry beads found among the natives of West Africa are Phoenician or Egyptian in origin and prove a trading connexion, by land or sea, between North and West Africa. A good deal of the east coast was known. At different times canals were attempted and sometimes completed between the Nile and the Red Sea. There was plenty of coming and going up and down the Red Sea, such traffic as a modern poet has described:

> Quinquireme of Nineveh from distant Ophir
> Rowing home to haven in sunny Palestine,
> With a cargo of ivory,
> And apes and peacocks,
> Sandalwood, cedarwood, and sweet white wine.

Ophir apparently was on, or included, some part of the east coast, and the coast was possibly known as far as the Zambesi, but the origin of the ruins found in Southern Rhodesia does not seem so far to have been determined. Finally, the map constructed from the writings of Ptolemy the geographer, who wrote about a century and a half A. D., shows the Nile flowing from two lakes, a very happy anticipation of the truth. But these early voyages and discoveries were no more fertile in result than the very much later but still comparatively early discovery of America by the Norsemen. The test of discovery is whether it stands for all time and all the world and leads to fresh discovery. Tried by this test, the man who completed the discovery of the African coasts was Vasco da Gama, and, more than any other man, the discoverer of the interior of Africa was David Livingstone.

*Africa in ancient history.* Broadly speaking, Africa in ancient times meant Egypt and the Red Sea littoral and the north coast of Africa. Ancient Egypt and the Egyptians is far too big a subject to be handled here; but two points may be *Egypt.* noticed. The first is that at every stage of the world's history, from the beginning of recorded time to the present day, Egypt has played an important part, especially in connexion with world empires. The Nile made it, as the rivers of Mesopotamia made Babylon and Nineveh, one of the rival great river empires. It came into the Persian Empire: it was prominent in the ancient Mediterranean world; and Alexander the Great occupied it, as is testified by the name Alexandria. It became a province of the Roman Empire, and later of the Turkish Empire. Napoleon, in his scheme for a world empire, held it for a moment. In the late war it came within the circle of the British Empire: with the cutting of the Suez Canal it gained new importance in relation to the whole world. There has been no time and no phase of civilization which has left Egypt out of account. The second point is that in the late war Egypt was what it was in earliest times, a base and starting-point for armed expeditions into Asia. In a sense Egypt was again marching against a Mesopotamian power, for the greater the pressure that was brought upon the Turks on the Egyptian side, the more their hold on Mesopotamia was weakened.

But while Egypt is at once a great river country and a Mediterranean country, with the north coast of Africa, west of Egypt, we come exclusively to the seaboard Mediterranean peoples, the Phoenicians, Greeks, and Romans. There was only one group of Greek colonies on the African coast, Cyrene and the adjoining cities, in what is now Tripoli. Cyrenaica passed under the Ptolemies of Egypt, a Macedonian dynasty, and subsequently into the Roman Empire. *North Africa.* *The Greeks.*

Prior to the Roman conquest of Carthage, the African coast west of Cyrene was Phoenician, the earliest Phoenician settlement on the coast being Utica, and by far the greatest, Carthage. The Carthaginians were the one and only people in ancient times who, hailing from Africa, made a great bid for a Mediterranean empire. In the Maltese the modern British Empire includes a people who claim Phoenician descent. The Phoenicians were the boldest seamen of the ancient world and the greatest traders. They went farther afield on the sea than any others, and nearly all the early voyages of adventure and exploration were in Phoenician ships and by Phoenician sailors. The one ancient European city outside the Straits of Gibraltar, Cadiz, was a Phoenician settlement. Sicily was the great meeting-ground and battlefield of Greeks and Phoenicians. In seamanship the Phoenicians may be likened to the Norsemen of the *The Phoenicians.*

early Middle Ages, but they had not the fighting pirate strain of the Norsemen. Although in the Carthaginian Hannibal they produced one of the greatest generals— some say the greatest general—of all history, they were a trading rather than a fighting people. Carthage went down before Rome, and Rome alone achieved an empire which covered the whole Mediterranean and the whole of Africa, so far as Africa was then known. Here it is worth noticing that the Roman Empire rested on land *Predomi-* power. It is true that the sea—not the outer but the *nance of* *land* inner sea—was the centre of the Mediterranean world. *power in* Empires or would-be empires, in the main, passed from *the Medi-* *terranean.* the great rivers to the shores of the inland sea. The map of the Mediterranean world is necessarily a map of water surrounded by land, and the coming and going between countries was mainly on the water. But none the less the land dominated the sea: it was not sea power but land power used on sea as well as on land that decided the mastery of the Mediterranean. The peninsulas took the lead, not the islands. Crete appears to have been great in prehistoric times, but in recorded centuries the islands of the Mediterranean ranked a bad second to the peninsulas. Sicily would indeed seem to have been marked out by nature as the seat of a Medi- terranean empire. It was—relatively—a very large island, with good harbours, and in a magnificently central position. But while it was always prominent in Mediterranean history, it never led. The final fight for the empire of the Mediterranean was between the two central peninsulas, Italy and Carthage, and Italy won, though Carthage had—on paper at any rate—con- siderable maritime power, and Rome had little or none. Why was this? Why was it that in this particular civilization, which centred round water, sea power did not predominate? The answer is given by Dr. Arnold in his history of Rome when he says, 'the naval service of the ancient nations was out of all proportion inferior to their land service'[1]. The Athenians seem to have been the only ancient people who made a real attempt at sea power in the true sense of sea power, that is, sea power depending, in war as in peace, upon seamanship; and the Romans apparently conquered the Carthaginians at sea by turning the sea fight into a land fight on sea. In ancient times the water was the one easy highway for traffic, but the command of the highway was secured, not by the most skilful seamen, but by the hardest fighters at close quarters, whether on land or sea.

Such were the Romans. No one thinks or writes of the Romans as a race of sea-dogs. They were emphatically landsmen and soldiers. But they were much more than mere fighters, or they could never have held the ancient world as they did. Gibbon says the Roman Empire was supposed to contain at its greatest time, the age of the Antonines, 1,600,000 square miles. Lord Bryce has put the area at 2,500,000 square miles. Anyhow it was smaller than Australia, much smaller than the Dominion of Canada. It seems to have touched the tropics at one point only—in Upper Egypt. The Romans, therefore, never dealt with the natives and problems of the tropics. West of Egypt the north coast of Africa was divided into two or three Roman provinces. The grouping differed at different times. It was in parts extensively colonized and highly developed. It was a great grain-producing section of the Empire, and it provided Rome with at any rate one strong emperor, Septimius Severus, who was born in Africa. Now,

*The Romans and their Empire.*

---

[1] *History of Rome*, 3rd ed., ii. 573.

keeping in mind the British Empire as it is to-day, and particularly in Africa, what was specially noteworthy in the Romans? They were essentially a military people, their power from first to last rested upon armed force. Not being by nature sea-goers, they gave no lead to exploration and discovery. Though we read of Nero sending an expedition to discover the sources of the Nile, the Roman Empire did not appreciably add to contemporary knowledge either of Africa or of the world. But the Romans had two great virtues. With all their militarism, all their oppressions and exactions, they were in administration by far the most modern and enlightened of the ancients, the most liberal, the least exclusive, and possessing the greatest sense of law. They were tolerant to different religions, they permitted and encouraged local liberties, and, as Mr. T. W. Arnold has well said, they were 'not cursed with the passion for uniformity'[1]. They were the one ancient people who, or the best of whom, as illustrated in Trajan's letter to Pliny, had real capacity for ruling. In the second place, if they were not pioneers in discovery, they were pioneers in disciplining and in civilizing barbarous lands. A striking evidence of their capacity for rule is the peace and cohesion which followed on the advent of the Roman eagles, and which was brought about largely through their system of public works. There were no road-makers like the Romans. We do not read of the Greeks, for instance, as perpetually making roads. The Romans, with their military instinct, thoroughly appreciated the value of communications. The water, as has been said, was the great highway for the ancients, and the Romans, landsmen as they were, well understood how to keep the highway

[1] *Roman Provincial Administration*, 1906 ed., p. 22.

open, to put down piracy, and to police the sea. But it was on land that their engineering qualities were most fruitful. Roman roads, bridges, and irrigation works remain to this day, and Roman colonies and colonists were to be found all over the ancient world. Freeman says that Roman civilization never took root in Africa to the same extent as in Gaul or Spain [1], but this statement is hardly borne out by the manifold traces of Roman civilization which have been and are being unearthed in North Africa, and it does not make allowance for the fact that Mohammedanism permanently annexed North Africa, while it had only a temporary though long lodgement in Spain, and hardly touched France. Now, if the question is asked how best may a backward continent be opened and redeemed, the answer surely is, by adjusting the incoming régime to the local conditions, by avoiding the 'passion for uniformity', and by giving public works and communications, in modern times pre-eminently railroads. In these matters the Romans were pioneers, and this it is that constitutes their surpassing greatness. Perhaps among modern peoples we resemble them most, except that we are far more of a sea-going people and far less of a military people than they were; so far as these last two points are concerned, the French, also great road-makers, are nearer to them than we are. It is the French who very especially have entered into the Roman heritage in North Africa. Freeman has written of the French occupation of Algeria and Tunis as 'the winning back from Islam of a land which once was part of Latin-speaking Christendom' [2]; and that they are worthy heirs of the Romans is illustrated by M. Jules Cambon,

[1] *Historical Geography of Europe*, 1882 ed., p. 61.
[2] Ibid., pp. 372-3.

who was Governor-General of Algeria. He had a conversation with a native on one of the old roads in Algeria known as Roman roads, and with reference to the term *Roumi*, applied by Arabs to Europeans, the Algerian said, 'Vous êtes bien les mêmes hommes que ces Romains, qui sont venus autrefois. Comme ceux, ce que vous faites le plus, ce sont des routes. Véritablement nous avons raison de vous appeler des Roumis. Voyez-vous, vous faites des routes et vous passez.' [1]

[1] *Le Gouvernement général de l'Algérie, 1891-1897*, Cambon, 1918.

## II

## AFRICA FROM ANCIENT TIMES TO THE
## NINETEENTH CENTURY:
## THE NATIVES OF AFRICA

In the fifth century A.D. the Vandals gained a tem- *The* *Vandals.*
porary footing in North Africa and in Freeman's words,
written before the entry of Germany into Africa,
'founded the one Teutonic Kingdom in that continent,
with Carthage to its capital'.[1]  This lasted for rather
over a century.  The Vandals came from and through
Spain, where the name Andalusia bears witness to
them, and in another passage Freeman writes of 'the
general law by which, in almost all periods of history,
the masters of Spain have borne rule in Africa or the
masters of Africa have borne rule in Spain'.[2]  If this
saying is tested by the present political position in
North Africa, support is given to the contention in the
last chapter that in the earlier Mediterranean world
land power predominated.  At the present day Spain
has an insignificant hold on North Africa, compared
with that of France, although France is removed from
Africa by the whole length of Spain ; but, until sea power
meant what it has come to mean in modern times,
Spain and Portugal had most to do with Northern
Africa, simply because in their case there was less sea
involved.  Note, too, that the quotations above from

[1] *Historical Geography of Europe*, ut sup., p. 92.
[2] Ibid., p. 81.

*The Historical Geography of Europe,* illustrate the fact already mentioned that the north coast of Africa was, more especially in ancient times, the southern fringe of Europe.

*The Arab conquest of North Africa.*
Across the Straits of Gibraltar the Arab conquerors of Northern Africa passed into and conquered the Spanish peninsula. They conquered North Africa, after having conquered Egypt, in the last half of the seventh century A.D., and the early years of the eighth. It was a complete conquest; the whole of Africa, as known to the Ancients, that is Egypt, and the north and east coasts of Africa, with the exception of Abyssinia, came under Arab domination. The Arab (the Saracen) must be carefully distinguished from the Ottoman (the Turk). Though they are all alike Mohammedans, the late war has borne out M. Jules Cambon's statement[1] with reference to North Africa twenty-five years ago, that the Turk had no worse enemy than the Arab. The Ottoman appeared in North Africa at a very much later date than the Arab, in the sixteenth century, and his overlordship in North Africa did not extend to Morocco. On the east coast Turkish claims were asserted, when in the eighties of the last century we constituted the British Somaliland Protectorate, at least as far as the Horn of Africa. They held the Hedjaz and Yemen in Arabia and thus dominated or claimed to dominate both sides of the Red Sea. It will be borne in mind that the Turkish power in Africa began and grew not before, but after, the modern peoples of Western Europe had in their turn begun to intrude into Africa. The point is important because, as will be seen hereafter, the modern history of Africa is not solely a history of

*The Turks.*

[1] 'Le Turc, par exemple, n'a pas de pire ennemi que l'Arabe.' *Le Gouvernement général de l'Algérie,* ut sup., p. 432.

European aggression and penetration into a passive continent. Other peoples contributed to the ferment, and the African races themselves pressed upon one another.

The coming of the Arabs was the beginning of the *Far-reaching effects of the incoming of the Arabs.* modern history of Africa. No one event, or series of events, so vitally affected the whole continent for all time. It swept Europe and Christianity from the north coast of Africa. North Africa now became not so much the southern fringe of Europe as the western end of Asia. M. Jules Cambon has described Algeria as in effect not a European but an eastern country.[1] Farther west than Algeria, Tangier, in Morocco, at the extreme north-west of Africa, is to all intents and purposes an eastern city. The Arabs on their camels passed on into the Sahara and across the Sahara into the Sudan. Accordingly, a map on the front page of the third volume of Mr. Beazley's *Dawn of Modern Geography* marks the southern limit of Moslem knowledge of 'the interior of Africa in the latter half of the thirteenth and the first half of the fourteenth centuries A.D. at a point about ten degrees north of the Equator, while on the east coast it extended much farther south, to a little below the mouth of the Zambesi. Within these limits the Arab left a lasting mark on Africa. Arab and Mohammedan penetration leavened the whole of the northern half of Africa, so that, very roughly speaking and allowing for exceptions, such as Abyssinia and the Copts in Egypt, Africa at the present day, down to about ten degrees north latitude, and lower down on the east coast, is in the main Mohammedan, while south of that line it is pagan or Christian. It has just been

---

[1] 'En effet l'Algérie n'est pas un pays européen mais un pays oriental.' *Le Gouvernement général de l'Algérie,* ut sup., p. 9.

noticed that there are divisions in the Mohammedan as in the Christian world, but probably it would be safe to say that Mohammedanism has brought more cohesion in its train than has Christianity, and that the spread of Mohammedanism tended to solidify Northern Africa as against Christian Europe. Moreover, the direct route to the East passed entirely under Moslem control. Hence came another result of the Arab invasion. Christian sailors and traders sought to avoid the Moslem barrier; and so the circumnavigation of Africa, and the exploration of the coasts of Africa, flowed directly from the Arab invasion of Africa.

*The natives of Africa.* Before speaking of the Portuguese and Vasco da Gama, it will be well to say a word of the native races of Africa. According to all the authorities there are few aboriginal inhabitants in any country. Almost always we are told that the peoples in possession originally came from somewhere else. In all the talk about white men taking the natives' land, it seems to be overlooked that the natives were and are, when left to themselves, perpetually taking each other's lands. History teaches us that the whole upward course of the human race has been accompanied by wholesale migration and intrusion, and it is the most difficult thing in the world to decide the rights and wrongs of the matter, to say who are or ought to be the owners of the lands, and how far their ownership should be respected. Did Australia belong of right to the comparatively few Australian natives? When white men went to North America, how far did it belong to the North American Indians, again comparatively few? These Indians were largely hunters, and for hunting forest and waste land is required. Ought great tracts of North America to have been kept out of cultivation because of native rights? Should those rights have prevailed against the growth of the United States? These are not merely academic questions. At the present day we are told in some quarters that all the evils of the world are due to capitalism, and that the British Empire is an embodiment and expression of capitalism—very especially in the dependent continent, Africa. Capitalism means making and accumulating wealth. Wealth is made either by producing something or by carrying and exchanging the product. Is it or is it not right to get the most and the best that can be won, either from the surface of or from underneath the earth, and to distribute it where it is wanted? If it is right, are the people who at a particular time occupy a particular bit of the surface of the earth to decide whether or not that bit should be left fallow? If what is called beneficial occupation of land is to be taken as the true test of ownership, how far are native rights of ownership to be respected, if obviously the best use is not being made of the land? No one can answer these questions, but at any rate we can be on our guard against wholesale generalization. Every case has to be tested on its merits and in the light of common sense.

Sir Harry Johnston, a very great authority on African races, seems to regard Asia as the original source and home of all the coloured African peoples, past or present. Presumably the dwarfish tribes or races were the earliest incomers, the nearest to what we should call aborigines of Africa. When the white men first came to South Africa, the natives whom they encountered were Bushmen and Hottentots. The Bushmen, one of the diminutive races, now all but extinct except in South-West Africa and Angola, were apparently of very old African descent. The Hottentots, now mainly found in South-West Africa, are supposed to be a mixed breed, Hamites with Bushman blood in them. In North Africa the Berbers in Algeria and Morocco, and the kindred tribes or races, appear to have held their ground throughout all history, while changing their religion. They adopted Mohammedanism from the Arabs. They are apparently classed by the best authorities as Hamites. Generally speaking, North and North-East Africa are peopled by Hamite and Semite races, with endless inter-mixtures. The Somalis appear to be comparatively pure Hamites ; the Semites include the Arab stock. The Egyptians are said to be mixed Hamites and Semites, so are the Abyssinians, but in different proportions. South of the Sahara, but well north of the Equator, we come to the main African race, the negroes, less mixed with the North African races as we go southward ; and *The Ne-* east and south of the negroes proper is a kindred race, *groes and* negroes but not undiluted negroes, the Bantus, with *Bantus.* endless groups and varieties, Bechuanas, Zulus, and the rest. All the South African natives, who used to be spoken of in books as Kaffirs, are Bantus. Finally, in the island of Madagascar, there is a Malayan strain in the population.

With the modern intrusion of the white men into Africa, the African natives, *par excellence*, the negroes and the Bantus, may be said to have come into light and into history. There are two points about them to be noticed. In the first place both races must be very strong and prolific. Beyond all peoples negroes were marked out by white men for slavery : they were marked out because they were strong. The wastage was terrible, the cruelty hideous, but the negroes maintained themselves in Africa, and, helped by the tropical climate, have turned the lands to which they were carried as slaves into negro lands. The killing out of the Bantus, both by themselves (as by the Zulu king Chaka, for instance) and by white men, was appalling; but in South Africa, where the climate suits the white man as well as the black, they have not died out before the white man. On the contrary, they are said to be multiplying faster than the Europeans.

The coloured races of Asia and Africa seem to be of much stronger physique than the natives of America, or of Australia and the Pacific Islands. But when Asiatics and Africans come into contact and competition, the Asiatic is in stamina apparently the stronger of the two. This deduction is made from the results of East Indian immigration into lands where the Africans have been beforehand. In the African island of Mauritius, in 1830, just before slave emancipation, over two-thirds of the total estimated population were slaves, principally Africans. Systematic emigration from India began after negro emancipation about five years later, and now out of a total population in the island, nearly four times as large as in 1830, over two-thirds are East Indian.

The second point is a reminder that Africa was not simply a passive continent when modern Europeans came on the scene. In particular the Bantus were in constant movement, pushing one another south, and ousting Hottentots and Bushmen. Thus when the white men came in from the south and moved north, they met people who were still moving south. On the other hand, in the earlier part of the nineteenth century, one Bantu people, the Zulus, sent out waves again in a northerly direction, with the result that the Zulu stock is found not only in Matabeleland but as far north as Nyasaland.

When the world began to move on from the *The Portuguese in Africa.* inland sea, the Mediterranean, to the open western ocean, it might be expected that the lead would come from the peninsula which lies between the Mediterranean and the Atlantic. Into this Spanish peninsula the Saracens had crossed from Africa in the early years of the eighth century, and in a very short time they overran the whole of it except in the extreme north, where are the mountains of Asturias. From this nucleus the Christian reaction began, and as the Moslems were gradually pushed south, Portugal came into existence as a separate state. The Mohammedans were driven out from the western, the Portuguese, side of the peninsula, much sooner than they were farther east. Lisbon was gained by the middle of the twelfth century, and rather over 100 years later, well before 1300, the whole of Portugal, as it now stands, was cleared. Thus Portugal became what it now is much earlier than Spain. Then there was a long interval of over 100 years, before, in the year 1415, the Portuguese crossed into Africa and took Ceuta, over against Gibraltar. Ceuta has been in European hands ever since, but in Spanish hands from the date when Philip II of Spain annexed Portugal, not having been recovered by the Portuguese when they regained their independence. At a much later date in the fifteenth century, long after their discoveries had extended far down the west coast of Africa, the Portuguese gained more footholds in this north-west corner of Africa, including Tangier. Tangier, like Bombay, came to Great Britain in 1662 as part of the dowry of Charles the Second's Portuguese wife, Catherine of Braganza, but the English found it expensive, and gave it up to the Moors some twenty years later. It is one of our lost possessions.

*Prince Henry the Navigator.* It has been said that the crusading spirit entered into modern discovery. This was certainly true among the Portuguese and Spaniards. A foremost figure at the taking of Ceuta was a son of the King of Portugal by an English mother, a daughter of John of Gaunt. This was Prince Henry the Navigator, the father of modern maritime discovery. He never went on exploring voyages himself, but, until he died in 1460, he was the moving spirit in Portuguese exploration on the west coast of Africa and in the islands other than the Canaries, which were already known. His ships discovered or rediscovered Madeira in 1420, and later the Azores and the Cape Verde islands. Cape Bojador, the bulging cape, where the currents had long barred progress, was doubled in 1434; in 1445 the Senegal was reached, and in that year or the next Cape Verde, the westernmost point of Africa, was rounded; then the ships came to the Gambia, and when the prince died they were half-way between the Gambia and Sierra Leone. What had carried the Portuguese forward, over and above Prince Henry's personality and inspiration, was that, in the course of their trafficking, they came across gold dust and negro slaves; and conversion of the heathen, especially of the negro (a much more amenable person to convert than the Mohammedan), became a convenient argument for slave-trading. Sierra Leone was reached just after Prince Henry's death; after a short interval all the coast of the Gulf of Guinea was skirted, and in 1471 the Equator was crossed and the ships reached the Ogove river. There was then a rather longer pause, but in 1484 the Congo was reached and the final stages followed. In 1486 Bartholomew Diaz sailed on southward, was blown by storm far to the south, and beating up again east and north, found that the coast was now running east. He had been blown round the Cape without knowing it.

He reached Algoa Bay and a little beyond, and sighted *The whole* the Cape on the way home in 1487. Ten years later, *African coast* in 1497, Vasco da Gama was sent out, doubled the *finally ex-* Cape, sailed up the east coast as far as Mombasa and *plored.* Melinde, then struck across the Indian Ocean, reached Calicut in India in May 1498, and after rather more than two years' time, came back to Lisbon in September 1499. Thus all the coasts of Africa were at last made known to Europe, the work having been done, and well done, by this one people the Portuguese. It will be noted that their progress was very gradual, and a great many years passed before they reached their final objective.

*Leading* Before Vasco da Gama started, Columbus had in 1492 *features in the* reached the West Indies. While Da Gama was starting *Portu-* in 1497, Cabot discovered North America. But because *guese ex-* Portuguese exploration was very gradual, it was, on the *ploration.* coast at least, very thorough. The place-names show this; the coast, especially the west coast, is plastered with Portuguese names. They tell how the explorers went on from point to point, Capes Bojador, Blanco, Verde, Palmas, Voltas, Cape of Good Hope (an English translation), Agulhas, Delgado, Guardafui. The islands were christened too.[1] But Portuguese names are not so plentiful on the eastern side north of present Portuguese East Africa. North of Cape Delgado the Portuguese found the Arabs before them. For the time they

[1] Teachers are strongly urged to make use of place-names in their teaching, and to include among them names of places which have been transferred to articles of trade and industry; e.g. Calico is derived from Calicut mentioned above, which was, when the Portuguese reached it, a great emporium of trade; Muslin is derived from Mosul near Nineveh, and so forth. See *Sir George Birdwood's Report on the Old Records of the India Office*, 1891, especially pp. 39-40 and notes and 224-5.

conquered the Arabs, but were eventually driven south again to their present limits. They went slowly to work, in part because, as they went, they traded, they made footholds, such as a fort on the bay of Arguin, and the great castle of Elmina on the Gold Coast, and they developed the islands. Religion went with them, to which place-names, telling of the Saints' days and, in the case of Natal, of Christmas Day, bear abundant witness, and in their later stages they were fired by the legend of Prester John. North of the Equator on the western side they seem to have had the strongest hold at Arguin, on the Gambia, and at Elmina on the Gold Coast. But their chief spheres were south of the Equator on both west and east, in Angola and Mozambique. Here they went furthest inland, and gained knowledge if not a command of the interior. They never did more than call at the Cape. Their very steady and gradual exploring work, in strong contrast to the Spanish rush into and over Central and South America, promised permanence ; but they were too small a people for what they had attempted and apparently achieved. Africa was with them subordinate to the East ; they never concentrated on Africa : and finally the sixty years' subjection of Portugal to Spain ruined the Portuguese Empire.

Other western European peoples followed where *The French in Africa.* Portugal had pointed the way. The French, or some of their writers, still claim that Dieppe sailors preceded the Portuguese in exploring the west side of Africa. Certainly a Frenchman was the first in modern times to make a settlement in the Canaries, as early as 1402. He owned the King of Castile as his overlord ; the islands soon passed to Castile and have remained in Spanish hands ever since. From the very first the region of the Senegal specially attracted the French.

They were most in evidence on that river and to a lesser degree on the Gambia : the Senegal country has always been peculiarly a French sphere, and in the Senegalese the French have perhaps the finest of all West African fighters.  Except for two or three years towards the end of the eighteenth century, they never had any footing on land on the Gold Coast, though their ships traded with that coast, and for two or three years at the beginning of the eighteenth century they had a station on the Ivory Coast, just west of the Gold Coast, at Assinie.  The French in early days had the reputation of being more tactful with the negroes than any other Europeans.

*The English.*   The English attempted to trade with the Guinea coast—the Guinea coast meaning in old times roughly the coast from the mouth of the Senegal to the mouth of the Niger—as early as 1481, before the Portuguese had reached the Cape ; but the ships were held up on a remonstrance from Portugal.  The first Englishman recorded as trading on the coast was William Hawkins, of the famous Devonshire family, father of Sir John Hawkins.  His venture was in the years 1530-2, and twenty years later, about 1553, a succession of Guinea voyages began.  The Gambia and the Gold Coast were always, until towards the end of the eighteenth century, the principal scenes of British enterprise in West Africa, the first British foothold on the Gambia possibly dating from 1618.

*The Dutch.*   The Dutch were later comers to West Africa than the French or English.  The first recorded Dutch voyage to Guinea was apparently not until 1595.  In 1617, a year before the founding of the British fort on the Gambia, they secured the island of Goree, off Cape Verde, and in 1624 they planted their first fort on the Gold Coast. The Gold Coast was their special attraction.

The Danes seem to have come to West Africa about the middle of the seventeenth century, and planted themselves on the Gold Coast, one of their forts, Christiansborg Castle, being the present residence of the British Governor of the Gold Coast. Finally, late in the seventeenth century, for about forty years, a Brandenburg or Prussian company had one or two forts on the Gold Coast which were sold to the Dutch. There was no subsequent German foothold in Africa prior to 1880. *The Danes and Branden- burgers.*

When the new worlds were opened up by the Portuguese and Spaniards, a Papal bull and the treaty of Tordesillas divided them between the two nations, and the Spaniards were thereby excluded from Africa with the exception of the Morocco coast and the Canary Islands. History took much the same course in Africa as in America. For fully a century, till after 1600, the Spaniards were supreme in Central and South America, except in Brazil, where the Portuguese had come in, and the Portuguese were supreme in Africa. Other Europeans traded either on sufferance or more generally as unlicensed interlopers. The people who broke the Portuguese both in Africa and in the East were the Dutch. They were at war with Spain and therefore with Portugal when, in 1580, Portugal was annexed by Spain. In 1637 they took the Portuguese castle of Elmina on the Gold Coast, and by the middle of the century the Portuguese were driven out of West Africa north of the Equator, except for the small section of the coast south of the Gambia which is still Portuguese Guinea and for the islands. Similarly on the east coast by 1700 they had been driven south, by the Arabs not *The Euro- peans in West Africa down to the battle of Water- loo.*

by Europeans, but they always kept Angola on the western side and Mozambique on the eastern, and they have them to this day. When the Portuguese had been driven out, the other Europeans in Africa, just as happened in America also, turned on one another. The Dutch, especially, having ousted the Portuguese, hoped to step into the former Portuguese monopoly. On the Gold Coast Dutch and English were the great rivals; farther north, in Senegambia, after the Dutch had been eliminated, French and English competed. The chief fighting between Dutch and English was in the great naval war in Charles the Second's reign, which ended with the Peace of Breda in 1667. It left the Dutch much stronger on the Gold Coast than the English, but after the war the English steadily gained ground. North of the Gold Coast the war between the French and the Dutch which followed in 1672 ended in the Dutch being replaced by the French in the island of Goree. Subsequently, in this northern section, during the various wars between France and England, the French and English footholds perpetually changed hands, but at the end, in 1815, it was very much as it was at the beginning, the French held the Senegal and the English in the main the Gambia. On the western side of Africa, the side on which in modern times Europeans came to Africa, before 1815 there are two special features to be noticed. The first is that no Europeans, except the Portuguese, had any permanent foothold from the mouth of the Niger—well north of the Equator—to the Cape. There was an English station for a while near the mouth of the Congo, but it was broken up by the Portuguese. The second is that on the West African coast generally, but especially on the Gold Coast, there were no colonies or dependencies in the ordinary sense, but just *pieds à terre* on the fringe of the coast for trade, mainly the slave-trade, as can be learnt from illustrations in old books such as Barbot's *Description of the Coasts of North and South Guinea*, which will be found in Churchill's collection of Voyages.[1] On the Gold Coast the forts and factories of the rival nations stood side by side with one another. At or near Accra, for instance, Danes, Dutch, and English all had forts. It was not a question of territory but of trade, and the first British attempt at a settlement or colony in the more ordinary sense was Sierra Leone, which dates only from 1787.

The Portuguese set out to explore the west coast of Africa in order to find a way round to the East, and the peoples who followed them to Africa followed them also to the East. But, as these peoples did not establish any post or settlement on the western side south of the Gulf of Guinea, so they had no foothold on the eastern side, though in the eighteenth century the Dutch from the Cape and later an Austrian Company from Trieste tried to form stations on Delagoa Bay. East Africa was left to the Portuguese and the Arabs until quite recent times. Vessels of all nations, coming and going between Europe and the East, called at the Cape, but the Portuguese never had any station there. In 1620 two English captains formally annexed it for King James the First, but the British Government refused to endorse their action, and it remained a No Man's Land, as far as Europeans were concerned, until at *The* length, in 1652, the Dutch planted themselves there. *Dutch at the Cape.* It was finally ceded to Great Britain in 1814. St. Helena, *St.* discovered by the Portuguese, was constantly visited by *Helena.* their ships, because it lies in the direct track of the

[1] 1732 ed., vol. v.

trade-winds blowing from the south-east, and therefore
in the direct track of homebound vessels from the east
and the Cape. It is said to have been occupied for
a few years by the Dutch, but, if so, they left it when
they had decided to form a station at the Cape, and
in 1651 the English took possession of it. Ascension
was occupied by us in 1815, and Tristan da Cunha
in 1816. On the eastern side of Africa the Portuguese
*Mauri-* discovered the various islands. The Dutch were the
*tius,*
*Bourbon,* first to make a settlement in Mauritius, in or about
*and* 1639, but left the island in 1712, and in 1715 the
*Mada-*
*gascar.* French occupied it, having already planted themselves
in Bourbon or Réunion about the same time as the
Dutch went to Mauritius. The French too from the
middle of the seventeenth century were persistent in
attempts to establish themselves in Madagascar, and
at the time of the Napoleonic wars they were the predominant people in the islands on this side of Africa.
The end of those wars gave to England Mauritius and
its dependencies of the Seychelles, Rodrigues, and
various small islands, gave back to France Bourbon,
and left French claims on Madagascar unchallenged
by England, though at the time the only permanent
French foothold in or near Madagascar was the little
island of St. Marie off its east coast. Mauritius may
be cited as illustrating the value of place-names in
teaching history. The island was so called by the
Dutch, long before their occupation, after Count
Maurice of Nassau. Under the French it was famous
as the Île de France, and the English took over what
was a thoroughly French island. But, by restoring the
name Mauritius, they recalled the fact of the obsolete
Dutch occupation.

It may be summed up that in 1815 the Spaniards held

Ceuta and Melilla on the Morocco Coast, the Canary Islands, and Fernando Po and Annsbon, which had been ceded to Spain by Portugal in 1778. The Portuguese held Portuguese Guinea, Angola, Mozambique, Madeira, Cape Verde Islands, Azores, St. Thomas and Principe islands. The Dutch had no holding except on the Gold Coast, neither had the Danes. The French held the Senegal country, the island of Réunion, and a foothold off Madagascar. The English were strong on the Gambia and on the Gold Coast, they were planted at Sierra Leone, and they held the Cape, St. Helena, Ascension, Mauritius, the Seychelles and Rodrigues. There were also various claims at different points and by different peoples, which were made the most of subsequently, but at the time they were indefinite claims; and so far hardly more than the outer rim of Africa had anywhere come under European control. This was the condition of affairs little more than a hundred years ago.

## III

## THE SLAVE-TRADE: SIERRA LEONE AND
## LIBERIA

IT was said in the first chapter that, while geography
and climate primarily accounted for keeping Africa so
long locked up, human agency also contributed to the
same result. Mohammedanism and the slave-trade, each
in its own way, helped to keep the continent a dark continent. Our present concern is with the slave-trade.

*Two kinds of African slave-trade.* There were two varieties of African slave-trade, the
slave-trade which was connected with the West Coast
of Africa, the infamy of which attaches to Europeans
and among them conspicuously to our own people, and
the Mohammedan, the Arab slave-trade, which was
mainly confined to the east coast, and against which
(after the days of the West African slave-trade)
David Livingstone began a crusade. The English were
especially instrumental in abolishing the east coast trade.
The first was more economic, the second was more
domestic. We are now to deal with the western slave-
trade, the slave-trade of history.

*Causes of the West African slave-trade.* In order to appreciate its origin and development we
must again look at the sea more than the land, at the
Atlantic Ocean fringed on the east by West Africa, on
the west by Eastern America. It must be borne in mind
that the exploration of the West African coast and the
discovery of the negroes immediately preceded the discovery of America. On the African side of the Atlantic
there was the barbarous negro race, among whom slavery

was indigenous, a physically strong race, well fitted for manual labour in the tropics. On the American side, on the contrary, the natives were by comparison few in number and either less tractable, as the Caribs, or far weaker in physique than the African negroes. It must be further borne in mind that, after an interval, during which the white man was establishing himself in tropical America and the West Indies, it was found that the soil, especially in the West Indian islands, was extraordinarily fertile for plantation products, and particularly for sugar.[1] These plantations needed a regular supply of manual labour, and it was not forthcoming on the spot. Barbados, for instance, has always been devoted to sugar growing, but when the English first went to the island it had no human inhabitants at all. Consequently, as a look at the map will show, to bring labour across from Africa was an intelligible proceeding. Thus a carrying trade grew up which, if the labour had been voluntary labour, and the conditions of the 'middle passage', as it was called, had been fit for human beings, would have been just as blameless as any other carrying trade. The importance of this carrying trade was increased by another circumstance. The Spaniards, who owned great domains in tropical America, had no place in West Africa, and therefore the other European peoples, not only carried for their own plantations in America, but also for Spanish America, and competed among themselves for the monopoly of supplying the Spaniards. This monopoly, the 'Assiento' or 'contract', as it was called, played an important part in political history, and one of the provisions of the Treaty of

[1] The sugar-cane is said to have been brought from the East to Madeira in 1420 and on to Hispaniola in 1494. See Birdwood, p. 109.

Utrecht in 1713 secured it to Great Britain for a term of years. It is therefore easy to see that what became an appalling crime, the worst blot by far upon English history, grew out of natural and coinciding causes.

*History of the slave-trade.* The first comers to West Africa, the Portuguese, were also the first slave-traders. In the early days of their voyages they bought negroes secondhand from the Moors; then they planted themselves on the coast of negroland and procured their slaves direct. Before the discovery of America some hundreds of negro slaves *The Portu-guese.* were brought back annually to Portugal; after the discovery hundreds became thousands and Lisbon set up a slave-market, for in the early days of the trade the negroes were shipped to America through Lisbon and not direct. The first negroes taken across were set to work in the mines of Hispaniola, where the Spaniards had largely killed out the natives; afterwards the plantation system grew up. The Portuguese monopolized the slave-trade for so long as they monopolized West Africa, till after 1600; and, as they were the first slave-traders, so they were almost the last. There is, or was till recently, something akin to slavery in the cocoa-growing Portuguese islands of St. Thomas and Principe, and remains of a slave-trade lingered long in Angola. Angola lies directly over against Brazil, which used to belong to Portugal, and no doubt this was one reason why the Portuguese always kept such a firm hold on Angola.

*The Dutch.* Brazil was one of the very few parts of the world where the Dutch, after a long struggle, were beaten off by the Portuguese. The Dutch took over the slave-trade from the Portuguese, along with everything else belonging to Portugal that they could lay their hands upon. They were essentially a nation of carriers, and the bitter rivalry between English and Dutch was a competition of peoples in the same line of business. Our Navigation Acts were primarily directed against the Dutch carrying trade. The Dutch, however, were more directly middlemen than the English. Systematic English slave-trading began with the supply of slave-labour to English colonies, and our countrymen then went on to carrying slaves generally, but the Dutch seem from the first to have aimed at monopolizing the general carrying trade, and down to the middle of the seventeenth century they supplied some British colonies, such as Barbados, with slaves.

The first record of British slave-trading, however, is *The English. Sir John Hawkins.* found long before there were any British overseas plantations[1] to supply with slave-labour. In 1562 Sir John Hawkins took some negroes from Sierra Leone and carried them to the Spaniards in Hispaniola. He repeated this slave-trading in other voyages, breaking into both the Portuguese and the Spanish monopolies. It will be remembered that his father was the first recorded English trader to the Guinea coast just thirty years before, and it is curious that English slave-trading began at the very place, Sierra Leone, where at a later date the first British settlement for freed slaves was planted. But Hawkins was a great deal more than a slave-trader. He was a foremost figure among great Elizabethan seamen and Treasurer of the Navy. There was a monument to him in the Church of St. Dunstan's in the East, but it was destroyed in the Fire of London.

[1] The word 'plantations' was originally used more with reference to the planting of human beings than of sugar, rice, &c. It was simply equivalent to colonies. Thus Bacon's short essay on colonizing is entitled 'Of Plantations', and the Government department which dealt with the Colonies in the eighteenth century was styled the Board of Trade and Plantations.

He had an office at Deptford, but there is no memorial of him in St. Nicholas' Church, the mother church of Deptford. It was not till about 1660, after the Navigation Act of that year had been passed against the Dutch, that the English entered fully into the slave-trade, and an African Company, which was granted a Royal Charter by King Charles II, and which included among its members the king's brother, afterwards King James II, contracted to supply 3,000 slaves annually to the British colonies in the West Indies. Slave-labour for the sugar plantations was by this time a fully recognized and firmly established system; a regular supply of negro labourers was demanded annually, and since they were to be supplied, it was not likely that the English would be content to leave the carrying of them, at any rate to English plantations, in the hands of the Dutch. But for some years to come the Dutch exported many more in all than the English.

*The French.* The French were not general carriers to the same extent as the Dutch, but at the end of the seventeenth century they exported a great number of slaves from West Africa. By the Treaty of Ryswick, in 1697, they obtained from the Spaniards the cession of the western part of the island of Hispaniola, which in Burke's *European Settlements in America*, first published in 1757, is called 'the best and most fertile part of the best and most fertile island in the West Indies and perhaps in the world'. In the *Wealth of Nations*, first published in 1776, Adam Smith wrote of it: 'It is now the most important of the sugar colonies of the West Indies, and its produce is said to be greater than that of all the English sugar colonies put together.' In 1726, according to the *European Settlements in America*, the French had over 100,000 negroes in the island. Apart from supplying

their own colonies, the French at the end of the seventeenth and the beginning of the eighteenth centuries,
before the power of Louis XIV was broken, held the
contract for supplying the Spanish colonies with slaves,
but this passed to Great Britain by the treaty of 1713.

In the eighteenth century the slave-trade was at its *The slave-trade in the eighteenth century.*
height, and the English became the greatest slave-
traders. In the early years of the century the English
export of slaves from Africa seems to have amounted in
all to about 25,000 negroes annually. In the latter part
of the century, after the Seven Years' War and the
peace of 1763, the total number of negroes exported by
all nations has been placed as high as about 100,000 per
annum, though various statistics are given ; and, on an
average, the English seem to have carried something
like half; the Portuguese, always great slave-traders,
also carried a large number. The English companies
which were successively formed for the West African
trade did not find slave-trading profitable, but that was
largely because private slave-traders cut into their
monopoly. The trade must have been lucrative or it
would not have held out so long nor died so hard. It
was the making of Liverpool. The first slave-ship
belonging to Liverpool sailed in 1709 ; by the end of the
century it is said that Liverpool did five-sixths of the
British slave-trade, and just before the trade was
abolished there were 185 Liverpool ships in the trade
carrying not far short of 50,000 slaves annually. Bristol,
which before the Norman Conquest had had a slave-
trade with Ireland, and London also dealt largely in the
trade.

The King of Denmark was the first to make the *Abolition of the slave-trade.*
slave-trade illegal for his subjects, in 1792. The first
resolution against the trade in the House of Commons

(it was not carried) was moved in 1776. A committee for its abolition was formed by Wilberforce and others in 1787; through their efforts an inquiry was held in 1788, and the report was presented to Parliament in 1789. In 1788, too, an Act was passed prescribing more humane conditions on the slave-ships. Leading statesmen pronounced against the trade, Pitt, Fox, and Burke among others, and at length in 1807 it was abolished by Act of Parliament. Another Act in 1811 made slave-trading a felony. It was swept away by the persistence of a few good men, among them Granville Sharp, Thomas Clarkson, and Wilberforce. They were upheld by religious bodies, especially the Quakers, by statesmen whom the country trusted, and finally, when the facts were brought home to them, by the innate humanity and good sense of the English people. The trade would never have lasted so long if it had gone on under their eyes, but the slaves were carried from Africa, not from England. By common consent Dr. Johnson, more than any one man dead or alive, embodies English humanity and good sense, and Dr. Johnson's Toryism did not prevent his hating and denouncing the slave-trade and slavery in every form and without any compromise or qualification. 'Upon one occasion (says Boswell), when 'in company with some very grave men at Oxford, his 'toast was, "Here's to the next insurrection of the 'negroes in the West Indies".' Sterne, writing in 1766, is equally emphatic. Thus in a letter to Ignatius Sancho, an American negro, after mentioning a 'tender tale of the sorrows of a friendless poor negro girl' which he intends to place 'at the service of the afflicted', he declares that he never looks westward in pensive mood, 'but I think of the burdens which our brothers and sisters are there carrying'.

Happily there is no need to give details proving *Moral aspect of the slave-trade.* the cruelty and the wickedness of the slave-trade, and but for the late war it would not be necessary to moralize on the subject. But the methods of barbarism resorted to in the war have shown how thin is the veneer of civilization, and how crimes can be and are supported by plausible arguments. Similarly, the atrocities in the Belgian Congo, well within the present century, prove what white men in pursuit of gain are capable of among African negroes. It is only 113 years since the English gave up slave-trading and much less than a century since, dating from the 1st of August, 1834, slavery was abolished in the British Empire. Since that date we can claim to have done far more than any other nation to put down slave-trade and slavery, and it is generally admitted that our race is not a cruel race. Still the fact remains that we slave-traded in the most wholesale and unqualified manner, and there is the further assertion made by English writers that the treatment of the slaves on British plantations was not better but worse than their treatment by other peoples, notably the French. This will be found in the book already quoted, *The European Settlements in America*, and Adam Smith refers to the French planters as treating their slaves better than the English. If this was so, the reason no doubt was the very interesting reason given by Adam Smith, viz. that the French West Indian colonies were more strictly controlled from home than were the British. The British West Indian colonies were largely self-governing and the laws and administration under which the slaves lived were the laws and administration of a white oligarchy in the midst of a much greater number of black men. Government from a distance, or rather

ultimate control from a distance, is a great safeguard
to native races; because it is less biased by colour
prejudice, and acts as a check on local authority. The
natives are quick to see this. When the Union of
South Africa was formed, the great fear in the native
territories was lest they should be removed from the
control of the Imperial Government and handed over
to that of the Union. A further disgusting aspect of
the bad treatment of the slaves was that mortality
among them increased the demand for fresh impor-
tations and therefore benefited the carrying-trade. So
one crime supported another. This point is touched
upon in *The European Settlements in America*.

It may fairly be said, in summing up, that the British
slave-trade is an appalling illustration of the strength
which vested interests can acquire, and of the extent
to which familiarity with crime can deaden the con-
science and blur discrimination between plain right and
wrong. The first British African Company was formed
for honest trade, and ships sent to the Gambia refused
to buy negro women offered for sale by a negro, on the
ground that Englishmen did not buy and sell 'any that
had our own shapes'. Honest trade went on subsequently side by side with trade in human beings, but
slave-trading became the mainstay of West African
commerce. Thenceforward there was no question as
to the morality of the traffic; the great issue was
whether it should be monopolized by a company or
thrown open to competition, so that, by free trade in
slaves, their price might be kept down. Thus an Act
of Parliament in 1750 recited that 'the trade to and
from Africa is very advantageous to Great Britain, and
necessary for supplying the plantations and colonies
thereunto belonging with a sufficient number of negroes

at reasonable rates, and for that purpose the said trade
ought to be free and open to all His Majesty's subjects'.
In the eighteenth century sugar-growing was more
profitable than any other form of production, the West
Indian colonies were at the height of their fortunes,
and the West Indian interest was most powerful in
England. The planters wanted to get their labour as
cheaply as possible. Slave labour had become a matter
of course, all European peoples slave-traded, and the
English declined to hand over their profits to others.
The Rev. John Newton, the friend of the poet Cowper,
as he afterwards was, was a mate and a master on
slave-ships before he became a clergyman. He became
'converted' while still slave-trading and read divine
service on his slave-ship. Apparently he did not find
religion incompatible with slave-trading. In after years
he was incumbent of the Church at the end of Lombard
Street, St. Mary Woolnoth, and on the wall is his
epitaph on himself, in which he describes himself as
'a Servant of Slaves in Africa'. He died in the same
year in which the Abolition Act was passed, in 1807.
James Boswell was a cultivated kindly man, but he
protested most strongly against Dr. Johnson's antipathy
to the slave-trade, and even ventured to regard it as
'zeal without knowledge'. He wrote of 'the wild and
dangerous attempt' to procure an act to abolish 'so
very important and necessary a branch of commercial
interest', and continues: 'To abolish a status, which in
all ages God has sanctioned, and man has continued,
would not only be robbery to an innumerable class of
our fellow subjects, but it would be extreme cruelty to
the African savages, a portion of whom it saves from
massacre or intolerable bondage in their own country,
and introduces into a much happier state of life,

especially now that their passage to the West Indies and their treatment there is humanely regulated.' It was a favourite apology for the slave-trade that slavery was indigenous among the negroes in Africa, but that was no reason why Europeans should encourage, share in, and profit by it. They did so, however, and these illustrations show how habituated to the system men's minds became.[1]

*Effect of the slave-trade on America*

But, leaving the moral side altogether, there are two other aspects of the slave-trade to be noticed, its effect on America and its effect on Africa. In its effect on America it was a great colonization movement. The West Indian islands and the present black belt of the United States, not to mention other parts of America, became, for good or ill, permanently settled by negroes. In reviewing and estimating the overseas work done by our British race—or indeed by any European people—stock should be taken not only of the extent to which we have colonized with our own race but also of the extent to which we have transplanted or contributed to transplanting other races. The slave-trade was in effect a great forcible transplantation, resulting in negro colonization on a very large scale. The abolition of slavery was followed by another transplantation, transplantation of East Indians, not a forcible but a voluntary transplantation, under contract, with a right to return. The outcome of this movement in Mauritius has already been

---

[1] The slave-trader himself disdained apologetics. Mr. Pope was with Sir Godfrey Kneller one day, when his nephew, a Guinea trader, came in. 'Nephew,' said Sir Godfrey, 'you have the honour of seeing the two greatest men in the world.' 'I don't know how great you may be,' said the Guinea man, 'but I don't like your looks : I have often bought a man much better than both of you together, all muscles and bones, for ten guineas.' (Dr. Warburton, *Spence's Anecdotes.*)

given. Through the same system British Guiana, Trinidad, Fiji, Natal, have in their population a very large East Indian element, and other British sugar-growing colonies have East Indians in smaller proportion. Finally Great Britain, simply by establishing her rule or protection over certain areas, has attracted a great amount of immigration from outside. Very especially has this been the case in the Malay Peninsula, where, owing to the presence of Great Britain and the added attraction of tin mines and other sources of wealth, Chinese and East Indians have swarmed in, and now in many parts of the Peninsula, under British control, far outnumber the indigenous Malays.

But we are mainly concerned with the effect of the *and on* slave-trade on Africa. Its effect, and it could hardly *Africa.* be otherwise, was to lock up Africa. Game preserves cannot be anything but locked-up lands, uncultivated and unopened areas. The West Coast of Africa was a great preserve for human game. It was a scene of barbarism when Europeans went there and of intent they maintained the barbarism. They did not want to form settlements and make roads inland. They only wanted fortified factories and accommodation for slaves by the sea-shore. Conversely, once the tide turned against the slave-trade, just as the crusading spirit called forth by Mohammedanism had given impetus to African discovery, so the crusading spirit against slave-trading had a precisely similar result. It was plain common sense that the most effective way to kill the slave-trade was, as Livingstone saw so clearly, to open up the interior and give facilities and security for honest trade. *The*

Before the western slave-trade was abolished, there *founding of a free* was a beginning of a better time in the foundation of *colony at* a colony for free negroes at Sierra Leone. Because *Sierra Leone.*

of its fine harbour and good supplies of wood and water, Sierra Leone was a great resort for the ships of all nations, for slave-traders and for pirates. The scheme for a free negro settlement in West Africa was the result of Lord Mansfield's famous judgement in 1772 that a slave on setting foot in England became free. In consequence of it a large number of blacks were turned adrift in London, some good men constituted themselves a committee for relieving the black poor, and, advised by a man who knew the Grain Coast, which was strictly speaking just south of Sierra Leone, in the present republic of Liberia, they decided to form a settlement for these destitute free negroes at Sierra Leone, the Government agreeing to pay the cost of transport. The philanthropists were not free from the vice of ordinary promoters and permitted themselves some little exaggeration of their pet scheme; their handbill described the scene of the future settlement as 'one of the most pleasant and fertile countries in the known world'. The enterprise was badly organized, and there was much delay; however, the first party of emigrants reached Sierra Leone in May 1787, a grant of land was obtained from a local chief, and rather over a year later, in August 1788, the native king of the country confirmed the grant by a treaty in which he swore allegiance to the king of Great Britain, thereby making it in effect a grant to the Crown. The neighbouring slave factories continued to carry on business as usual during all this time. In 1791 a Sierra Leone company was incorporated by Act of Parliament for opening up trade with the interior in connexion with the new settlement, and in the Act the ground which had been ceded was spoken of as vested in the Crown. The first settlement was broken up and the survivors were restarted on a new site, which was called Granvilletown after Granville Sharp, but when a large number of blacks, who had gained their freedom by taking the British side in the War of Independence, was brought over from Nova Scotia in 1792, the old site was reoccupied and the settlement was called Freetown. It was looted and burnt by a French republican squadron in 1794, when Zachary Macaulay, father of the great historian, was governor, but subsequently made steady progress and is now the capital of the Colony. An account of the early years of the settlement and of its spoliation by the French will be found in Sir George Trevelyan's *Life and Letters of Lord Macaulay*.[1] There were constant difficulties, largely owing to the great mixture of black settlers, including Maroons[2] from Jamaica. In 1800 the Company was given a Charter of Justice, which made over the ceded land to them subject to a nominal rent to the Crown, and the whole power was placed in their hands. But they did not succeed, and in 1807, the year of the abolition of the slave-trade, a new Act was passed, Sierra Leone was constituted and has remained ever since a Crown Colony, and the Sierra Leone Company was merged in the African Association, to which

---

[1] Vol. i, chap. i.

[2] The word Maroon is said to be short for Cimaron or Symaron, from Cima, a mountain-top, and means mountaineer. The Jamaica Maroons were in origin runaway slaves from the Spaniards, while the latter held the island. They always maintained their freedom, and late in the eighteenth century a Government report dealing with the slave-trade speaks of 'the four free negro towns' in Jamaica. There was at times much trouble between them and the Government, and Maroon wars; some of them were temporarily deported, hence their presence at Sierra Leone. There were Maroons in other colonies also, notably, in French times, in Mauritius.

further reference will be made. Thus, coincident with the abolition of the slave-trade, was established the first Crown Colony on the West Coast of Africa. It owed its origin to the two kindred objects of freedom and the development of trade with the interior of Africa.

*The founding of the Liberian Republic.* The founding of Sierra Leone inspired the founding of Liberia, which is its immediate neighbour on the south-eastern side. The full story of Liberia is given in a recent book, *The Republic of Liberia*, by Mr. R. C. F. Maugham, late British Consul General in the Republic. It originated with a philanthropic American Colonization Society, formed in or about 1816, just as Sierra Leone originated with English philanthropists, and Sierra Leone was the base and starting-point for the first American attempts at a settlement for freed slaves in West Africa. In 1818 agents were sent to make inquiries, the first party of emigrants came across apparently in 1820, land was acquired at Cape Montserrado, or, as it is now called, Cape Mesurado, and in 1822 a settlement was established there. The names of Liberia and Monrovia, its chief town, called after President Monroe, author of the 'Monroe Doctrine', came into use in 1824. The settlement at first was independent of the American Government, which had a separate agency in Africa appointed under an Act of Congress of 1819 to receive freed slaves, but soon the head of the settlement seems to have been also the Government agent. The matter is rather complicated, but the details are given in *The Suppression of the African Slave Trade to the United States of America*, by Dr. Du Bois, published in the Harvard Historical Studies Series in 1896. The settlement was controlled by an agent of the Colonization Society, who was subsequently made governor and given a Council; sometimes the governor was a white man and sometimes a coloured. The Society gradually left the settlers more and more to manage themselves and finally relinquished all control in 1846. In 1847 the Liberians made a high-sounding declaration of independence on the lines of the American Declaration of Independence and proclaimed themselves a sovereign republic. It was immediately recognized by Great Britain, France, and other European Powers, but not till some years later by the United States. A separate settlement, emanating from Maryland and called Maryland, had been planted farther south in the neighbourhood of Cape Palmas. This was amalgamated with Liberia in 1857. Mr. Maugham gives a very roseate picture of Liberia, but as a matter of fact it has been a travesty of a state, chronically bankrupt and undeveloped. We are told in his book that there are about 14,000 or 15,000 American Liberians, and 30,000 to 40,000 of mixed Liberian stock, out of a total population of 600,000 or 700,000. It has, in fact, been a kind of negro oligarchy on or near the coast, purporting to rule a territory about four times the size of Belgium, the interior of which is, or was till quite lately, not even known. Before the late war there was some kind of international control of the finances of the Republic by the United States, Great Britain, Germany, and France, but the United States have now taken over sole charge and obligation. It would have been very much better if the American Government had from the first acted as the British Government did in regard to Sierra Leone, and either annexed Liberia or placed it under definitive American Protectorate and control. Liberia has been an object lesson in the disadvantages of self-determination for the negro race as contrasted with tutelage by the white man. Its territory, as already stated, covers what was known as the Grain Coast, the grain being the Guinea pepper, a kind of spice, and the native Africans of this section of the coast are the seamen of West Africa, the Krumen or Kruboys.

*The beginnings of modern exploration of Africa.*

One of the first of modern explorers in Africa was James Bruce, who, in 1770-2, visited Abyssinia, discovered the source of the Blue Nile and traced it down to the confluence with the White Nile at Khartoum. He was one of the very many Scotsmen whose names are associated with the opening up of Africa. Some years later, in 1788, just at the time when the Sierra Leone Settlement was founded, an African Association was formed for exploring the interior of Africa. About

*The African Association.*

forty years later the Association was merged in the Royal Geographical Society. They sent out in 1795 another great Scottish explorer, Mungo Park, who made his way from the Gambia to the Niger, reaching the Niger at Segu, high up on its course. In 1805 he was sent out again, this time by the Government, went up once more from the Gambia to the Niger and died in trying to follow the Niger to the sea, the place where he died being Bussa, very far down the river, within the borders of the present Nigeria. Park had formed the view that the Niger would come out as the Congo, and before his day, in the middle of the eighteenth century, there was an impression that the Senegal and the Gambia were both mouths of the Niger.[1] What is important to bear in mind is, first, that until the nineteenth century was well advanced, hardly anything was

[1] The *Annual Register* for 1758 stated ' The river Niger, according to the best maps, rises in the east of Africa, and, after a course of 300 miles nearly due west, divides into three branches, the most northerly of which is the Senegal as above, the middle is the Gambia or Gambra, and the most southern, Rio Grande '.

known of the centre of Africa, less than seems to have been known, either by hearsay or from personal exploration, to the Portuguese 150 or 200 years earlier; and secondly, that the crusade against the slave-trade and exploring enterprise went on simultaneously and had a direct bearing the one on the other.

## IV

## MISSIONARIES AND EXPLORERS:
## DAVID LIVINGSTONE

DAVID LIVINGSTONE died in 1873. Before treating of his work and that of other explorers, which bore its full fruit later in the 'Scramble for Africa', as it has been called, it will be well to sum up what changes in or additions to European tenures in Africa were made between 1815 and 1873. On the West Coast, the French steadily extended their area in Senegambia both on the *Extension* coast and inland, though very much more gradually and *of European hold-* slowly than in the last fifty years. There was a rather *ings in* important Franco-British Agreement in 1857. Prior to *Africa* that date the English had a treaty right to trade—it was *to 1873.* a trade in gum—on the coast north of the Senegal, from the mouth of the river St. John to the bay of Portendik. In turn the French construed their treaty rights as entitling them to keep their old fort or factory at Albreda, on the Gambia. The 1857 agreement cancelled these rights or claims against each other, leaving the French in undisputed control of the coast region of the Senegal and the English undisputed masters of the Gambia. On the Gambia, what was really the first permanent British settlement, in the ordinary sense, had been made in 1816, on St. Mary's Island at the mouth of the river. It was called Bathurst after Lord Bathurst, then Secretary of State for the Colonies, and his name appears as a place-name in various parts of the Empire, his chief title to fame being that he was Colonial Secretary for a longer time continuously than any Colonial Secretary before or since, the next longest tenure of the office being that of Mr. Chamberlain. Subsequently to the founding of Bathurst the British area was extended on the Gambia, including McCarthy's Island higher up the river. Similarly there was extension at Sierra Leone. Below Sierra Leone, on the Grain Coast, we have seen that Liberia came into being as a black, not as a white, settlement. Below Liberia, and after turning the corner at Cape Palmas, was the Ivory Coast. Here, as has been stated, at the beginning of the eighteenth century, the French had had a station at Assinie, which they gave up. About 1843 they came back, and though it is not clear whether even then they remained in continuous occupation, from that date onward they never lost their hold on this section of the coast. Next comes the Gold Coast. Now in West Africa (with the exception of Sierra Leone), and very especially on the Gold Coast, for fifty years or more from the battle of Waterloo, the British Government, in contrast to the French, was perpetually chopping and changing its policy, and more often trying to contract than to extend its area of rule and responsibility. As late as 1865 a Select Committee of the House of Commons made a report contemplating the ultimate withdrawal of the Government from West Africa, with the exception of Sierra Leone. But facts made any such policy impossible, and very soon afterwards, far from withdrawing from the Gold Coast, the English became sole masters on that Coast. The Danes had already been bought out in 1850, and in 1871 a treaty was made with the Dutch by which they also were eliminated [1] in the following year, 1872. Thence-

[1] The wording of the Convention of 25th February 1871, by which the Dutch gave up their rights and possessions on the Gold Coast

forward neither the Danish nor the Netherlands Government retained any foothold in Africa. On the east of the Gold Coast is what was known as the Slave Coast. Here again the French obtained some kind of footing at Porto Novo, which, as in the case of Assinie, lasted permanently. At the eastern end of the Slave Coast there was a nest of slave-traders at Lagos, and eventually, having tried unsuccessfully to root out the trade, Great Britain in 1861 took possession of the town. It is now the great port of Nigeria. This annexation was carried out four years before the House of Commons report, which deprecated taking up any fresh responsibilities in West Africa.

Turning south, past the as yet unappropriated Niger Delta into the Bight of Biafra, and noting as we go that the Baptist missionaries, who settled at Victoria, Ambas Bay, on the Cameroon Coast in 1858, had anticipated subsequent European intrusion, we come to Corisco Bay and the Muni River. Here Spaniards, probably from Fernando Po, gained some rather indefinite holding, which, as with the French on the Ivory Coast and the Slave Coast, became subsequently defined and formally recognized. Immediately south of Muni, in or about 1842, the French definitely planted themselves on the Gaboon River, and some twenty years later on the

---

to Great Britain, is noteworthy. The Convention stated that 'the mixed dominion exercised on the Coast of Guinea by Great Britain and the Netherlands has occasioned to the native populations much harm . . . and the remedy for which is not to be expected until the two Powers shall carry out, with regard to their respective possessions, the principle of abstaining from or giving up mixed dominion or mixed possession'. The *quid pro quo* was contained in a separate Convention on 2nd November 1871, by which Great Britain gave up certain British rights in the Dutch island of Sumatra. This was one of many instances of Africa being brought into international barter.

Ogove. Apart from these there is no further change till we come to South Africa. Here, between 1815 and 1873, there was a very marked increase of European penetration inland. The great trek of 1836, due largely, though indirectly, to missionary influence, of which more will be said hereafter, led to the founding of Natal, the two Boer Republics, and to a wide extension of the Cape Colony. Basutoland was annexed and so was Griqualand West, with the Diamond Fields. In 1872, the year before Livingstone died, the Cape Colony became self-governing; thus by this date the curtain had gone up on modern history in South Africa. On the East Coast, above Natal, except that Delagoa Bay was confirmed to Portugal as against Great Britain by Marshal MacMahon's award of 1875, in all those years there was no change in or addition to European tenure until the Red Sea is reached. Here, in 1862, the French bought Obock on Tajoura Bay, over against Aden, but did not actively occupy it till the 'eighties. After securing Aden in 1839, the English acquired some small islands in that bay and made treaties against foreign intervention on the Somali Coast immediately opposite to Aden. There was an interesting 'might have been' in 1824. The captain of a British ship, at the urgent request of the natives, declared a British Protectorate over Mombasa and the adjoining coast, but, as happened at the Cape in James the First's reign, the Government would not endorse his action.

On the north coast of Africa there was a European intrusion in this period, of first-rate importance. Algiers had for two centuries and more been a head centre of piracy. The corsairs, or Barbary pirates, lived upon plunder of the Mediterranean shipping, the perpetual wars and jealousies of the different nations preventing concerted *The French annexation of Algeria.*

action against them. Turkish authority over Algeria had long disappeared, and it was an independent community of pirates and Janissaries with a nominal head called a 'Dey'. All nations, including the Americans, suffered, and after Waterloo the Powers talked of putting down the nuisance. In 1816 an English squadron under Lord Exmouth, with some Dutch ships, bombarded Algiers. Subsequently, on fresh provocation, the French took decisive action, and a French expedition occupied Algiers in 1830. There followed a very long war, the French being faced by a most gallant and skilful leader, Abd El-Kader, who did not surrender till the end of 1847. This was the beginning of a permanent recovery for Europe of the North African coast, as distinct from such isolated holdings as that of Spain at Ceuta. Thus began too the great modern French Empire in Africa, linking up north and west.

Finally, the year 1869 saw the opening of the Suez Canal. This meant indirectly a great strengthening of the European hold upon and interest in Africa, and it provided a new and much shorter waterway to East Africa, which, while the only sea route was round the Cape, had been the side of Africa most remote by water from Europe. In 1875, through the purchase of the Khedive's Canal Shares by Lord Beaconsfield, Great Britain obtained a predominating voice in the control of the canal.

*African exploration between the days of Mungo Park and Livingstone.* Thus, between 1815 and 1873, by far the most definitive and substantial European advance in Africa was on the north and from the south; but, before Livingstone's time, exploration was most active from the west and from the north. Mungo Park's journeys had proved that the Senegal and Gambia were not mouths of the Niger, but it still remained to be proved that the

Niger did not run into the Congo mouth, and what was the exact locality of the mouth of the Niger. In 1816, presumably to ascertain whether or not the two rivers were connected, the British Government sent out two expeditions, one to the Upper Niger in the direction which Park had taken, the other to the Congo, but both failed. Then came an expedition from the north coast, from Tripoli, in which the leading figure was another Scotsman, Clapperton. He discovered Lake Chad in 1823 and visited the now familiar Sultanates of Northern Nigeria, Sokoto, and Bornu. On a second expedition, in 1825–7, starting from the west coast near Lagos, he reached the Niger at Bussa, where Park had died, paid a second visit to Sokoto, and there died. In 1830 the brothers Lander, who had been with Clapperton, followed the Niger down from Bussa to the sea and found that the Oil Rivers, already known to traders, were the Niger delta. Thereafter merchants, especially Liverpool merchants, now engaged in honest trade, did exploring and trading work up the river from its mouths. Meanwhile, again from the north, Laing— another Scottish name—reached Timbuktu in 1826, and a Frenchman, Caillé, reached it from the west in 1828. At a later date, to mention one more great explorer, the German Dr. Barth (a member, and the only member who survived, of an expedition sent out by the British Government, again from Tripoli on the north coast) in 1851–5 visited Timbuktu, Lake Chad, and Northern Nigeria, going farther and making more minute investigation of the countries which he visited than any who had gone before him. His journey coincided with the great east and west trans-African journey which brought world-wide fame to David Livingstone. But Barth's was a journey which rather amplified existing discoveries than made new ones.

By the time when Queen Victoria began her long reign Europeans had crossed the Sahara and visited Timbuktu, the course of the Niger had been determined, and the first of the great African lakes, Lake Chad, had been discovered. Take a map of Africa of about this date and it will be seen what a contrast there is between this section of the continent and the great blank space farther south. It should be noted how entirely the opening up of the interior of Africa has been a matter of finding and following up lakes and rivers, and it should also be noted that this earlier wave of exploration started from the west and north, from the two coasts which, though nearest to Europe, had been locked up, the one by the slave-trade, the other by religious fanaticism. Undoubtedly the crusade against and the final abolition of the West African slave-trade gave the exploration both motive and impetus. It showed too how the resulting commercial loss caused by the abolition of the slave-trade might be made good by opening up the interior to ordinary traffic.

*David Living-stone.* We now come to the final lifting of the curtain. David Livingstone had sixty years of life. He was born in 1813, two years before the battle of Waterloo, and died in 1873, two years after the Franco-German War. He was born in Blantyre near Glasgow, was sent as a boy to a cotton-mill, earned his living and educated himself, resolved to become a missionary, attended classes at Anderson's College and the University in Glasgow, took a medical diploma, was ordained a missionary for the London Missionary Society, left for South Africa at the end of 1840 and joined Dr. Moffat, whose daughter he subsequently married, at Kuruman, then a remote

mission centre in Bechuanaland, north of the Cape
Colony. He began travelling almost directly and took
up mission work farther north among the Bechuana
tribes in what is now the Bechuanaland Protectorate.
His first notable discovery was that of Lake Ngami,
which he reached in company with his friend and bene-
factor, Oswell, and another companion, Murray, in 1849.
In 1851, again with Oswell and taking his family, he
visited the Makololo and their chief, whose centre was
on the Chobe river near its junction with the Zambesi,
in what was afterwards known as the Caprivi Strip
of German South-West Africa, and he went on to the
Zambesi itself. He made great friends with these
Makololo, as he did with all natives, and went back to
them alone in 1853. After exploring for some distance
the Upper Zambesi, he decided to find a route to the
west coast and reached it at Loanda at the end of May
1854. After some months on the west coast he went
back by more or less the same route to his Makololo
friends, then struck eastwards down the Zambesi, discovered the Victoria Falls, close to which the present
capital of Northern Rhodesia (Livingstone) stands, and,
following the river downstream, reached Quilimane on
the east coast in the latter part of May 1856. This
crossing of Africa from coast to coast made his name
famous for all time, apart from his subsequent achieve-
ments, and it was the pioneer journey of all the discoveries which rapidly followed. He went home to
England, severed his connexion with the London
Missionary Society, and, early in 1858, commissioned
by the Government to explore Eastern and Central
Africa and holding consular authority, he started for the
Zambesi. He was out till 1864. He thoroughly
explored the Lower Zambesi, the Shiré river and Shiré

Highlands, and Lake Nyasa, which he discovered in
September 1859, though it was possibly already known
to Portuguese travellers.  He also explored the Rovuma
river.  The chief settlement in the Shiré Highlands is
called Blantyre after his birthplace, and the range of
mountains east of Lake Nyasa is known as the Livingstone range.  Among his companions at this time was
Dr. Kirk, afterwards Sir John Kirk, of Zanzibar fame.[1]
This second turn of African exploration was not as
unqualified a success as the trans-African journey.
Livingstone lost his wife, efforts at establishing missions
failed, though Nyasaland subsequently became and now
is a great missionary field, and there were various
elements of discord and disappointment.  Meanwhile,
before he had left England on this second venture and
eighteen months before he discovered Lake Nyasa,
Richard Burton, with Speke for his companion, starting
from Zanzibar and, guided by Arab reports, in January
1858 discovered Lake Tanganyika, and Speke pushing
north, alone, in July 1858 sighted the Victoria Nyanza.
Speke was persuaded that here was the source of the
Nile and, with Grant, started again from Zanzibar in the
autumn of 1860, reached the Victoria Lake a year later,
and in July 1862 found the outlet of the Nile.  He was
told of the Albert Nyanza, but not allowed to visit it.
He made his way down to Gondokoro on the Nile in
February 1863 'and so home.  At Gondokoro he met
Sir Samuel Baker, gave him the information as to the
unvisited lake, and going on up the Nile, Baker, in
March 1864, discovered the Albert Nyanza and proved

---

[1] Old and blind, he died 15th January 1922.  To the last he was
fond of exhibiting certain arrows discharged by the natives at
Livingstone's boat as it slowly worked its way up the Rovuma,
and which he picked up off the deck and preserved.

that the Nile flowed into and out of it. Thus, when
Livingstone came home in 1864, the Nile problem had
at length been solved, but it still remained to be proved,
whether its ultimate source had been reached, whether
the Victoria and Albert lakes were or were not connected with Lake Tanganyika, and the whereabouts of
the source of the Congo.

Mainly to determine whether there was any connexion
between the more southern lakes and the Nyanzas, and
whether the Nile had headwaters farther south than
Lake Victoria, Livingstone started alone on his last
journey in 1865. He reached Zanzibar early in 1866,
went up the Rovuma river, to the south end of Nyasa,
then on to Tanganyika, and there explored principally
in what is now Northern Rhodesia. He discovered
Lakes Moero and Ban weolo, the Chambezi, and the
Lualaba, persuading himself apparently to his death that
these rivers, which become the Congo, were feeders of
the Nile, just as Mungo Park thought that the Niger
would come out as the Congo. He was found by
Stanley, in the autumn of 1871, at Ujiji on the eastern
side of Tanganyika, close to Kigoma, which the Germans
afterwards made the terminus on Tanganyika of
their railway from the sea at Dâr-es-Salaam. With
Stanley he explored the north of Tanganyika and
verified that no river ran out of the lake at that end.
He had already proved that Nyasa was not connected
with Tanganyika, but he still clung to the belief or hope
that the rivers west of Tanganyika were feeders of the
Nile, and, with the supplies and men sent up by Stanley
from the coast, he went back to the region of Bangweolo
and died there in 1873. In that same year Lovett
Cameron, sent out by the Royal Geographical Society to
bring further help to Livingstone and aid in exploration,

met Livingstone's servants bringing his body down to
the coast. He went on to Tanganyika, found the outlet
of that lake, on the western side, the Lukuga river,
reached Nyangwe on the Lualaba river, the point which
Livingstone had reached, and satisfied himself that he
was on the Congo. He was unable, however, to follow
the course of the river, and eventually, in November
1875, he arrived on the west coast, much south of the
mouth of the Congo. It was left to Stanley, in the years
1874-7, to follow the Lualaba down from Nyangwe to
the sea, and finally to prove that it was indeed the
Congo. Thus all the main features of the African
interior were decided, and almost immediately followed
the ' scramble for Africa '.

*Leading features in the last stages of African exploration. Livingstone and his work.* In this short summary of the final unveiling of Africa
there are one or two leading features to be noted. In
the first place, as has already been insisted, it proved to
be a matter of finding and tracing waterways, and doing
it at first from the south, then from the east, whereas
earlier exploration had been from the north and west.
This was, of course, more or less inevitable, because it was
the more southerly and, on the whole, the more easterly
regions of Africa that were the least known. Still
nothing was done by following up the Congo from the
west, and the source of the Nile was not discovered
from the north, but from the east. In this final act the
eastern side of Africa comes greatly into prominence,
and Zanzibar becomes a great starting-point and jumping-off place, British influence, exercised from India,
being all-powerful there. In the second place, the
rapidity with which the final discoveries were made
stands out in extraordinary contrast to the interminable
length of time which elapsed before they began to be
made. Thirty years more than covers the whole

achievement from the date when Livingstone first sighted Lake Ngami to the time when Stanley came out at the mouth of the Congo. It is nearly always so. When the fullness of time comes, previous unrecorded or half-recorded spadework becomes of value, information collected and compared is ready to hand, and events move more and more quickly. Moreover, in the middle of the nineteenth century facilities for travel were multiplying and the world was becoming more accessible. But in this particular case there were two special and inter-dependent quickening influences at work. One was the Arab slave-trade, the other was the personality of the man who led the crusade against it, Livingstone himself.

On the eastern side of Africa, as on the west, the suppression of the slave-trade and the opening up of the continent went hand in hand. Purged herself from the crime, Great Britain led all nations in fighting the slave-trade. British ships policed the East African coast, intercepting the slave-vessels and, when Living-stone bore witness to the horrors of the trade inland, he had the British Government and British nation solidly behind him in the work of opening up Africa. When he made his famous journey to the west coast, he had praise for the Portuguese in Angola and seems to have thought that in this quarter the slave-trade was dead. If that was so at the time, the evil revived later and it has been suggested that his own journey to the West Coast had the result of opening up a slave-route. He had a very different tale to tell of the Portuguese traders on the eastern side and of the Arabs, and his life was thence-forward devoted to the two objects, inseparable in his mind and in their influence on each other, exploring and making known the interior and killing out the slave-trade.

We have seen that he started as a missionary, but
that he severed his connexion with the Missionary
Society and became more purely an explorer.  Early in
his career he was ill content with the standardized
methods of making and tabulating so many conversions,
real or nominal, annually.  He wished to know Africa
and the Africans, in order to clear a field for Christianity,
where it might grow naturally when savagery had been
weeded out ; and, when he was hampered in his work
by the slave-trade, he saw that the remedy lay not in
preaching but in revealing and reporting upon dark
places and dark deeds and by substituting a humane
for an inhuman traffic.  He tells us in a letter which is
given in Martineau's *Life of Sir Bartle Frere*, that, when
Lord Palmerston wanted to know how he could serve
him, instead of asking for anything for himself, he replied
that if Lord Palmerston 'could open the Portuguese
ports in East Africa to free trade, this was the greatest
boon he could confer'.[1]  We shall see hereafter that
opening to trade may, in turn, bring abuses in its train,
but none the less it was the immediate onward path.

Because Livingstone, with his breadth of view and
strong common sense, advocated commerce and inter-
course, it must not for a moment be thought that he was
unmindful of his missionary calling.  To the end he was
a missionary in the best and highest sense.  If ever a
man literally walked with God, it was Livingstone.
Perhaps the nearest parallel in this particular respect
was another man with a Scottish name, who also died
in and for Africa, General Gordon.  No other African
explorer won to the same extent as Livingstone the love
and admiration of the natives.  He could not have gone
where he went or achieved what he did without their

[1] 1895 ed., vol. ii, p. 116.

goodwill. Even the Arabs, or some of them, were good to him. He went year after year through wild Africa and among wild Africans with his Bible; he died kneeling at prayer, his native boys read the Burial Service, embalmed his body as best they could, and carried it with his few belongings for hundreds of miles to the coast to be taken home. Is there any record elsewhere in travel of so great a tribute of loving faithfulness? Livingstone, said his friend Sir Bartle Frere, 'was intellectually and morally as perfect a man as it has ever been my fortune to meet, one who formed vast designs for the good of mankind and placed his hopes of achieving them in no earthly power '.[1] Is it wonderful that a man of this type, coming when he did, and uniting behind him the forces of religion, of philanthropy, of science, and love of adventure, carried forward, almost with a rush, the final stages in the opening up of Africa?[2]

He was a Scotsman and a missionary. We have seen what numbers of Scotsmen there are in the list of African explorers, and it would seem that Scotsmen are as zealous in forwarding the cause of the next world as they are successful in controlling the affairs of this. Apart from definitively Scottish missionary societies, such as the Glasgow Missionary Society, which began work in South Africa about 1821, the London Missionary Society, which was still earlier in the field, abounded in Scottish missionaries, among them Dr. Moffat. We have seen, too, that the Evangelical school of Christianity

*Missionaries and the Empire.*

---

[1] *ut sup.*, vol. ii, p. 118.

[2] A very admirable account of Livingstone and his work is given in *Livingstone as an Explorer*, an Address to the University of Glasgow on the occasion of the Livingstone centenary in 1913 by Professor J. W. Gregory, D.Sc., F.R.S., and published by MacLehose and Sons. Its value is increased by the maps appended to it.

took the lead in fighting slave-trade and slavery, and,
coincident and connected with the fight, as the eighteenth century ended and the nineteenth century went
on its course, there was a great wave of evangelical
fervour in the mission field, the effort being rather
specially directed to Africa and the Pacific. The
missionaries became, and always have remained, great
champions of the native races, but not always wise or
scrupulous champions, and a classic instance of unwisdom
on their part occurred in South Africa just before
Livingstone went out, the missionaries concerned being
members of the society which sent him out and the
prime mover being a Scotsman, Dr. Philip. It is a long
story, very well known and constantly being retold. The
bald facts are that the Dutch in the Cape Colony were
restive and ill-content for various reasons, for instance,
because they were awarded inadequate compensation
for the emancipation of their slaves and because of endless difficulties and delays in getting the money. But
the climax of it all came when, after a most serious
border war and Kaffir invasion in 1834-5, the governor
annexed to the Cape Colony the adjoining Kaffir territory, and the Secretary of State for the Colonies at the
time, Lord Glenelg, a great philanthropist, was persuaded by Dr. Philip and his friends and supporters to
cancel the annexation and order the territory to be given
back. The result was what was known as the Great
Trek and the founding of the Dutch republics inland,
in effect the splitting up of South Africa. The Dutch
emigrants went off full of bitterness against the Society,
by which they held they had been slandered, they bound
themselves to have no dealings with it, and their temper
was shown a few years later, when a party of Boers
attacked the native Bechuana Settlement where Living-

stone was then working and, in his absence, looted his house.    Missionary influence in this instance was mischievous in the extreme, it poisoned the whole subsequent history of South Africa, and the mischief has never been undone.

But the particular point which it is desired to emphasize is the folly of the proceeding in the interests of the natives themselves.   Where native territories are unprotected, white men, unless they are prevented, are certain to intrude and to acquire claims and concessions. The natives are never strong enough to prevent them, and the one and only effective safeguard both for the natives and their lands is to do what the governor of the Cape did and take them under the British Government, which is strong enough to deal with white interlopers. Missionaries have not been slow to grasp this fact, and in consequence have usually been more on the side of expansion than of contraction of the Empire.   The case noticed above was almost an isolated instance of missionary influence procuring the withdrawal of British rule, and even so the influence was due to one Society alone.  Other missions at work in South Africa at the same time, such as the Wesleyan and Glasgow missionaries, did not associate themselves with the policy of Dr. Philip and the London mission.   It must not be thought that because this particular matter has been selected for criticism, mainly on account of its disastrous and far-reaching results, there is any ground whatever for belittling missionaries and their work.  On the contrary, they should be held in high admiration, especially in connexion with Africa.  At all points they have laboured, in the main with singular success.   To the various missionary bodies is due the advancement, industrial as well as spiritual, of the native races of Africa.   The present writer holds that the extension of the British Empire in Africa has been good for the coloured men, by placing them in tutelage under comparatively honest and considerate trustees; and it must not be forgotten that missionaries, no less than traders, have contributed to this end and been in a marked degree pioneers of the Empire.

# V

## THE SCRAMBLE FOR AFRICA, 1884-1891

### *The Belgian Congo ; The Entry of Germany ; Chartered Companies*

At the time when Stanley verified the course of the Congo, and the interior of Africa in its main features became finally known to the world, only four European nations (not counting the Turks as a European nation, and excluding the Boer states) had possessions on the continent, Spaniards, Portuguese, French, and English. The Spaniards had very little footing. The Portuguese had long fallen from their high estate, but still owned much territory and claimed more, on the west, Angola, and, much farther north, the small tract of Portuguese Guinea, on the east from a little below Delagoa Bay to Cape Delgado. The two active and progressive Powers in Africa were the two old rivals, France and Great Britain. Both had various holdings on the West Coast, neither had any on the east coast from north of Natal to the mouth of the Red Sea and hardly any there. On the north coast France was firmly planted in Algiers ; Great Britain, on the contrary, had no place. In the south France had no footing, while Great Britain was unchallenged except by the Boer republics inland.

In giving the date of Livingstone's life and death, it was pointed out that he was born two years before Waterloo and died two years after the Franco-German War. There was a reason for mentioning these wars. Each of them for the moment crushed France, and *Importance of the Franco-German War as a prelude to the scramble for Africa.*

after both the French, with their wonderful power of recovery, set themselves to gain new ground, to compensate for what they had lost, and, since they were already established in Africa, very naturally they looked there for new gains to set off the old losses. Thus the immediate prelude to the scramble for Africa was not only the discoveries which gave something to scramble for, but also the Franco-German War, and this for two reasons. The war unified Germany, and history would seem to teach that, when a country has achieved its own salvation and stands erect and free, it discovers a mission to spread that salvation to less favoured lands; unity at home is followed by expansion abroad. For example, the union of Aragon and Castile and the conquest of the Moors was speedily followed by the Spanish-American Empire. Our own Empire arose after the island of Great Britain had at length been united under one Crown. The United Netherlands gave birth to a great Dutch Empire overseas. United Germany obeyed the law, not through the designs of statesmen, for Bismarck was not in love with oversea ventures, but under pressure of public opinion. United Italy, one of the great results of the Franco-German War, followed suit and joined in the rush into Africa.

The second reason has been mentioned already. France wished to recoup herself for the loss of Alsace-Lorraine, and Africa, where she was already well placed, was an obvious and open field. Further, there was this important factor in the situation. While Germany took good care of herself in the parcelling out of Africa, German statecraft, in the earlier stages of the scramble, was by no means hostile to French claims and aspirations in Africa. They tended to distract French attention from their lost provinces at

home, and to result, as they did result, in renewed
rivalry between France and Great Britain, and in a
diversion of French bitterness from Germany to Great
Britain.  Moreover, they made bad blood between
France and Italy, and this again suited German designs.

Before the scramble began, France and Italy were *Assab and*
the first two Powers to gain ground in Africa during *Tunis.*
the memorable decade of the 'eighties.  The year 1880
is usually given as the date when Italy secured her
first African foothold, at Assab Bay, north of the French
Obock on the Red Sea coast.  In 1881 the French
greatly extended their position in North Africa by
declaring a Protectorate over Tunis, adjoining Algeria—
a Protectorate which the Italians, who had strong
interests in Tunis, bitterly resented and for a long
time refused to recognize.  But other intruders were
about to take the field.

In September 1876, while Stanley was on his journey *The be-*
across Africa, Leopold, King of the Belgians, called *ginning*
a meeting at Brussels of geographers, explorers, and *Belgian*
philanthropists, who agreed to form an International *Congo.*
African Association for exploring and civilizing Africa
and putting down the slave-trade.  The King himself
became President of the Association.  It was in no
sense a meeting of Government representatives, but
well-known men from most of the leading European
nations, including Great Britain, took part in it.  It was
decided that a national committee in each country
should collect money for the common cause.  As a
matter of fact, these national committees for the most
part went to work on their own account, and such
money as was collected was principally Belgian money
and mainly subscribed by King Leopold.  The Association met again in 1877 and adopted a flag, and one or

two unsuccessful expeditions were sent out. But before 1877 ended Stanley came home, having achieved his object and cleared up the Congo mystery; the King at once tried to get into touch with him, and did so at Brussels in June 1878. In November 1878 it was decided to establish a special committee, styled the Comité des Études du Haut Congo, which was apparently at first regarded as a branch of the International Association; plans were made, a small fund was raised, and Stanley went back to Africa as the committee's representative. So far the international character of the proceedings was maintained, and the money subscribed was not entirely Belgian money. But, even before Stanley reached the Congo, the foreign subscriptions were being returned and the enterprise was passing exclusively into the hands of the King of the Belgians, though there was still an international flavour in the scheme and indeed the committee later took the title of the International Association of the Congo. Stanley arrived at the mouth of the Congo in August 1879 and went up the river exploring, making treaties with native chiefs and founding posts. He returned to Europe in August 1882, was persuaded to go back to the Congo in the following December, and came back again to Europe in June 1884, his position, which was now tantamount to that of a Governor, being taken by an Englishman of high character and standing, Sir Francis de Winton.

*The French and De Brazza.* The Congo Committee had not been left alone in the field. A French explorer, De Brazza, had, in the years 1875–8, crossed from the Ogove into the Congo basin, but had not reached the Congo itself. He went back to France, went out again at the end of 1879, commissioned by the French Government and the French

Committee of the International Association, struck the
Congo in 1880 and, like Stanley, whom he met but kept
in the dark as to his proceedings, made treaties, obtained
concessions, and founded posts.   He arrived back in
France in the summer of 1882, later in the year the
French Parliament endorsed what he had done and
voted money to confirm his work, and this it was that
sent Stanley back to the Congo at the end of 1882.
Eventually the French maintained themselves on the
northern bank of the Middle Congo, and the Congo Association and what came out of it held the southern bank.

In old days the only European Power that had *The*
interests in the coast region of the Congo was Portugal. *Anglo-*
*Portu-*
The Portuguese had discovered the mouth of the river, *guese*
*Treaty of*
and for a time a native kingdom of the Congo was *1884.*
a great scene of Portuguese 'penetration' and of missionary enterprise.   Later the Portuguese left the
Congo and concentrated farther south in Angola, but
as late as 1783 they built a fort at Kabinda, north of
the mouth of the Congo (from which they were within
a year ousted by the French), and they consistently
maintained a claim to the coast as far north as 5° 12′
south latitude, thus including the mouth of the Congo
and Kabinda.   This claim was as consistently opposed
by Great Britain, who would not admit Portuguese
rights north of Ambriz in 8° south latitude.   Great
Britain was especially concerned in the matter because
she was especially interested in putting down the slave-
trade.   The activities of Stanley and De Brazza alarmed
the Portuguese, and again they pressed for a recognition
of their claim.   After negotiations, which began in
November 1882, Great Britain and Portugal signed
a treaty in February 1884, by which Great Britain
recognized the Portuguese claim on the coast, giving

her the mouth of the Congo and a certain distance
inland short of where Stanley had been operating, but
insisting that the navigation of the Congo should be
free to all nations. To this end the Congo was placed
under an Anglo-Portuguese Commission, the Portuguese
having refused an International Commission, which the
British Government originally suggested. This treaty
roused universal opposition. British merchants and
philanthropists strongly objected to extending the
Portuguese sphere, the French Government at once
refused to accept the treaty, the Congo Association
obviously did not want Portugal to have the mouth
of the river; the Germans supported the French. The
Portuguese, seeing that the treaty was doomed, turned
to France and Germany with a suggestion for an
International Conference; the treaty was formally given
up; Germany, in concert with France, in October 1884,
invited an International Conference to meet at Berlin.
It met in November, and eventually the famous General
Act of the Conference was signed on the 26th February
1885.

*The General Act of the Berlin Conference.* This Berlin Act, which was signed by all the Powers
interested in Africa and others also, fourteen Powers in
all, was a most important step, and full of promise for
the future. It provided for freedom of trade in the
widest sense in the Congo basin and for free navigation
of the rivers. It also provided for a wider free trade
zone, extending to the Indian Ocean, but conditioned
by the consent of any independent state within the zone.
It provided for the neutrality of the Congo basin which
was placed under international protection and surveil-
lance, for the well-being of the natives, and for prevention
of slave-trading. It provided, too, for free navigation of
the Niger, and it enacted that Powers making future

annexations in Africa must give due notice to other Powers, and that their occupation must be effective. The Berlin Conference was supplemented by later Conferences, the first and most important of which was the Brussels Conference of 1889-90, which was called by King Leopold and which passed a General Act, dealing mainly with slavery and the liquor traffic.

Before the General Act of Berlin had been signed in *The Inde-* February 1885, all the Powers which signed it had *pendent* *State of* given formal recognition to the International Association *the Congo.* of the Congo, the first to do so being the United States; and the boundaries of the Association had been partially fixed, in agreements with Germany, France, and Portugal. A few months after the signing of the Act, on the 1st August 1885, the formation of the Independent State of the Congo with King Leopold for its sovereign was announced. Thus a private association had developed into a state, whose neutrality was guaranteed by an international agreement, and whose king was the King of the Belgians in his personal capacity. It was not in any sense at this time a dependency of Belgium.

It will be convenient to follow out the further evolution of this State, before turning to the rest of the scramble for Africa. In 1889 King Leopold made a will bequeathing his sovereign rights to Belgium. In 1890 Belgium agreed to make a loan to the State for ten years on condition of being allowed to annex it at the end of that time. By this date, in 1890, Stanley had carried through his last great work of African exploration, the Emin Pasha relief expedition, traversing Africa from the Congo basin to that of the Nile and discovering Lake Albert Edward. In 1894, after new treaties with France, Portugal, and Great Britain, the boundaries of the State were defined afresh, and a further declaration of neutrality was made for the zone within those boundaries. Both before and after 1894 the King perpetually extended his territory, getting into and out of difficulties with Germany, France, and Great Britain, and making difficulties among those Powers. He pushed into the Nile basin, where he secured two leases of territory from Great Britain, one of which, on the western bank of the Upper Nile, known as the Lado enclave, was for his lifetime only.

*It becomes the Belgian Congo.* In November 1908 the State was at last transferred to Belgium, and became a Belgian dependency, the Belgian Congo, and the King died at the end of 1909. When the war came the exact eastern frontier of the State was at one point being delimited in accordance with a tripartite agreement, arrived at in 1910, between Belgium, Germany, and Great Britain, and one result of the war has been to extend, under a mandate, the territory at this end. An important point to be borne in mind is that from the first France secured the right of pre-emption of the Congo, and this French right was recognized when the State was taken over by Belgium. Thus by the ambition and ability of one unscrupulous man who was quick to see and to seize chances of playing off the rival Powers against each other, and to take advantage of the international basis of the State, a private association, originally formed for scientific and philanthropic purposes, gave birth to an immense dependency of a very small European country. Curiously enough, Belgium owed its own existence to certain of the same Powers which recognized and guaranteed the Belgian Congo. Belgium has an area of under 12,000 square miles, and the Belgian Congo before the war had an area of over 900,000 square miles.

The King's ambitious schemes necessarily meant *The Congo* great expense, there were obvious sources of wealth in *atrocities.* the Congo State, especially rubber, and in the effort to provide revenue and accumulate wealth, care for the natives and freedom of trade were disregarded, and from about 1895 onwards the most appalling abuses gradually came to light.   Large concessions were given to companies with whom the government went into partnership, the natives were deprived of their lands, forced to labour, taxed unmercifully, and treated with horrible cruelty.   The system, or want of system, became, in Lord Cromer's opinion, the worst he had ever seen, and Sir Edward Grey declared that the State had ' morally forfeited every right to international recognition '.   The British Government, Parliament, and people pressed for reform.   Public opinion in Belgium gradually became alive to the abuses and, indeed, at the outset of the evil, the then Governor-General, a Belgian, resigned.   With the taking over of the Congo by Belgium, and after King Albert, who had visited the Congo, succeeded King Leopold, there was real amelioration, and it is to be hoped that the administration will continue to improve.

The atrocities were beyond all question, but it will be sufficient here to emphasize some features without going into details.   In the first place, the evils must primarily be laid at the door of King Leopold himself. He seems to have run a kind of Rake's Progress which would have made him, had he been a private individual, a criminal of the not unfamiliar and not uninteresting type, moved at first probably by good or mixed intentions, urged on by ambition into more and more unscrupulous courses, and finally altogether losing count of justice and humanity.   In the second place, what happened in the Congo State should be regarded and studied as in some sort a parallel to what happened when the Spaniards discovered America. Central Africa was another New World, and Europeans ravaged and ruined the African in a manner which recalled Spanish savagery in earlier times. Thirdly, just as the Spaniards had had no previous experience of dealing with native American races, so it was with the Belgians in Africa. They, as also the Germans, were wholly new to Africa and the Africans. The behaviour of Portugal proves that long experience may fail to prevent maladministration, but familiarity with native races and native problems and a heritage of precedents and traditions is a very great help towards wise ruling. Belgians were set to administer an enormous territory without any training whatever. Fourthly, the record of the Congo does not support those who maintain that the salvation of native races is to be found in Internationalization. There was no concerted action to put down the abuses, in spite of a representation made in 1903 by the British Government to the other signatories to the Berlin Act ; and finally, if a text is needed either against Chartered companies, or against Governments taking part in trading concerns, it will be found in the story of the Congo.

We have seen that the great Conference of 1884-5 was invited by Germany in concert with France, and that it was held at Berlin. In other words, the Power which took the lead in the meeting so vitally concerned with the destinies of Africa was a Power which, prior to the 'eighties, owned no African possession whatever. Individual German explorers, missionaries, traders, had long been active in Africa, but until 1884, the actual year of the Berlin Conference, the German Government had no definite footing on the continent.  Then the German Government and the German nation not only made an entry into Africa, but from the first played a leading rôle.  In order to understand how this came about, we must bear in mind what was happening at the time in Great Britain.

In 1880 Mr. Gladstone swept Lord Beaconsfield out of office and came into power, as an opponent of the imperialism of the late Government.  The beginning of his term was marked not only by no further aggrandizement, but by an actual retreat.  There was withdrawal on the Afghan frontier, and, in Africa, retrocession of the Transvaal in 1881, after the Boer War and Majuba. Then came the Nationalist rising in Egypt, and in 1882, after a proposal to France for joint intervention, which France refused, there came British intervention in and military occupation of Egypt.  We no doubt intended to come out of Egypt again as soon as possible, the Government gave their word to that effect, and there is no reason to doubt their good faith.  But Egypt could not be left to anarchy, and the British occupation became indefinite, involving the most bitter feeling in France against Great Britain.  Thus it came to pass that, whereas, among the European Powers which had territorial interests in Africa when Germany came on the scene, Spain, Portugal, France, and Great Britain (Italy, as we have seen, having hardly begun her African career), the only one which could have offered effective opposition to Germany was Great Britain, at the precise time when Germany was assuming a conspicuous place in the African sun, the Government of Great Britain, notwithstanding its avowed principles and pledges against aggrandizement and annexation, became deeply involved in Egypt, as it already was in South Africa.

*Great Britain in the early 'eighties.*

The position was embarrassing and even damaging, for it attracted towards Germany the only other strong Power in Africa, France. This is the key to what followed.

*The entry of Germany.*   German missionaries had for many years been at work among the natives of South-West Africa, north of the Orange river. German traders followed, and there came a demand for the protection of these German subjects. In 1877 Sir Bartle Frere had advocated annexing the whole of the coast from the Orange river up to the Portuguese boundary, but nothing was done beyond annexing the harbour of Walfish Bay in 1878. Bismarck, urged by his countrymen, put it to Great Britain whether she did or did not claim the coast, and whether she would or would not take responsibility for the security of the Europeans in this region. There was a long interchange of notes, neither Great Britain nor the Cape Colony was willing to shoulder the responsibility and expense, and no definite answer was given, with the result that, in August 1884, a German Protectorate was formally proclaimed over South-West Africa. In the previous month, July 1884, the German flag was hoisted in Togoland and in the Cameroons, and, before 1884 ended, Germany had got her foot into East Africa, though as yet no German Protectorate had been formally proclaimed on this side. Great Britain, throughout, was reluctant to take any forward move, anxious to eschew any appearance of jealousy of a new-comer, and content to assert the existence of British interests at this or that point, without taking really effective steps to safeguard those interests, either by annexation of, or Protectorate over, the region in which they had grown up. Thus, before the Berlin Conference, Germany was firmly planted in Africa, and by summoning the Conference, she showed that she did not mean to play second fiddle there. So the scramble came to pass ; it remains to trace the results upon the map of Africa, in the barest outline, up to and including 1891.

We have seen that on the north coast, between 1880 and 1884, France had acquired Tunis and England had come into Egypt. On the Red Sea coast Italy had planted herself at Assab, and in 1883 the French entered into active possession of Obock. The collapse of Egypt involved the collapse of Egyptian authority in the Sudan, on the Red Sea littoral, and on the Somali coast. On part of this coast Great Britain had, in September 1877, recognized Egyptian jurisdiction, provided that the Turks, as suzerains of Egypt, concurred, which the Turks never did. On the Red Sea the Italians, in 1885, occupied the port of Massowah farther north than Assab Bay, and in the next three or four years consolidated their province now known as Eritrea. In 1884 the French from Obock obtained from the Sultan of Tajoura a cession of his country, and in 1888 Great Britain and France agreed as to a boundary line between their protectorates, the British giving up all claims on Tajoura Bay and ceding to the French the islets which they owned in the bay. Before this agreement, in 1884-6, Great Britain had made treaties with various Somali tribes over against Aden, and in 1886 had declared a Protectorate over the island of Socotra. In 1887 the British Somaliland Protectorate was formally declared, extending on the coast from the French boundary to the forty-ninth meridian of east longitude. This Protectorate was at first under the India Office, Aden being a dependency of India, and the eastern side of Africa, up to this time, being specially connected with India.

*The partition of Africa, 1884-1891.*

*North-East Africa.*

Bordering the British Somaliland Protectorate, and including the Horn of Africa, came Italian Somaliland, another Italian Protectorate, which was proclaimed in 1889, and which extended down to the Juba river, taking in what was known as the Benadir Coast. At its southern end this Protectorate intruded into the dominions of the Sultan of Zanzibar, and into territory which he had conceded to the Imperial British East Africa Company. The claims were adjusted and Great Britain and Italy came to an agreement in 1891, in which year also the two Powers came to an agreement on the Red Sea coast. But at this time Italian ambitions were not confined to the coast-line, and Italy claimed to have secured some kind of Protectorate over Abyssinia. If this had come to pass, the two Italian Protectorates would have been linked up inland and would have encircled the French at Tajoura and the British in Somaliland.[1] But it will be seen later that this far-reaching plan came to nothing.

*East Africa.* We are now to consider central East Africa. From the point last dealt with to the northern boundary of Portuguese East Africa, stretched the dominions of the Sultan of Zanzibar. It was an Arab sultanate, and the seat of the sultanate had originally been at Muscat in Arabia. Great Britain was the European power on which the Sultan leaned, and the able British representative at Zanzibar at the time was Livingstone's friend, Sir John Kirk. The Sultan a few years previously, in 1873, had signed an anti-slave-trade agreement, the Englishman who negotiated it being Sir Bartle Frere, and his foreign relations were *de facto* guided by the Government of India. After German intrusion had

[1] This Protectorate over Abyssinia is shown on the map facing p. 516 of Scott Keltie's *Partition of Africa* (1895 ed.).

begun to make itself felt, Lord Granville, in January 1885, stated plainly that 'for the greater part of the present century the sultans of Muscat and Zanzibar have been under the direct influence of this country and of the Government of India'. In 1877 the Sultan offered to Sir William MacKinnon, the head of the British India Company, a concession of the whole of his mainland coast-line, but the British Government would not take up the offer. In 1884 Germany began to secure a footing in East Africa. Here, as elsewhere in Africa, Great Britain pleaded special interests, but did not claim Protectorate. Moreover, while it was certain that the coast-line belonged to the Sultan of Zanzibar, it was not certain how far his dominions stretched into the interior, where the Germans had been busy making treaties and gaining concessions. To shorten a long story, in 1885 a joint British, French, and German commission was appointed to decide the exact limits of the sovereignty of Zanzibar, the British commissioner being the future Lord Kitchener. The Commissioners reported in 1886. In 1886 Great Britain and Germany agreed on respective spheres of influence in East Africa, and the Sultan, acting throughout very reluctantly on the advice and pressure of the British Government, accepted the arrangement. In 1887 the Sultan gave a concession to a company formed by Sir William MacKinnon and his friends, which, in 1888, received a Royal Charter as the Imperial British East Africa Company. In 1888 he ceded administration in the German sphere to a German company, and in 1889 a German Protectorate over the German sphere was formally proclaimed. Finally, in 1890 the great Anglo-German treaty was concluded, which settled the main boundaries between Great Britain and Germany in all the parts of Africa where the two nations were side by side, and under which, as against the cession of Heligoland to Germany, Great Britain secured German recognition of an exclusive British Protectorate over what still remained under the rule of the Sultan of Zanzibar. The French had joined the British and Germans in the Commission for deciding the limits of the Sultanate of Zanzibar. The *locus standi* of the French was that, in 1862, they had joined with the British in guaranteeing the independence of Zanzibar. France had not, and has not, any territorial interest on the eastern side of the African continent south of the Red Sea, but has always had interests and claims in the island of Madagascar. At the end of 1885 a French Protectorate over Madagascar was proclaimed, and in 1890 both Great Britain and Germany recognized this Protectorate, while France recognized the British Protectorate over the islands of Zanzibar and Pemba, and the German Protectorate in East Africa. On the south, German East Africa was coterminous with Portuguese East Africa and there was no difficulty as to the boundary, which was fixed, roughly, at the Rovuma river.

We have seen that, when the Anglo-Portuguese Congo treaty failed, Portugal turned round and made approaches to Germany and France. In 1886 she made *South* omnibus treaties with both these Powers, defining the *Africa.* respective boundaries in Africa generally. Both treaties conceded a claim made by Portugal to all the intervening territory between Portuguese East and Portuguese West Africa, the outcome of which would have been to give her an immense belt right across the continent north and south of the Zambesi, including Mashonaland and Nyasaland, and to bar effectually British expansion from the south. A map, showing Africa in these regions

as wholly Portuguese, was laid before the Portuguese
Parliament and will be found reproduced in Hertslet's
*Map of Africa by Treaty* (1909 ed., vol. ii, facing p. 706).
In 1887 the British Government strongly protested.
The tide of ill-success had now turned in South Africa,
and Great Britain was again moving forward. In 1885
Bechuanaland had been annexed and a Protectorate,
the Bechuanaland Protectorate, proclaimed farther
north up to the 22nd degree of south latitude. In 1889
the British South Africa Company was incorporated by
Royal Charter, and in 1890 established itself in Mashonaland. In that year a kind of British ultimatum was sent
to Portugal; there was much friction between the two
Powers, but eventually, in June 1891, a comprehensive
treaty was signed which secured to Great Britain
Nyasaland and the Rhodesias, and became the basis of
all future Anglo-Portuguese relations in Africa.

On the western side of Africa, it has been said that *West
Africa.*
the German South-West Africa Protectorate dates from
1884. The Anglo-German treaty of 1890 added to it an
additional narrow tongue of land, known as the Caprivi
Strip, of much importance to the Germans, as giving
them access to the Zambesi. The Germans settled with
the Portuguese their northern boundary in this region
in the general treaty between Germany and Portugal of
1886. The negotiations and agreements in connexion
with the formation of the Congo State conceded the
Portuguese claim northward up to and including the
southern bank of the mouth of the Congo, and on
the coast north, but not immediately north, of the mouth
of the river, gave them a small enclave, which they had
always claimed, at Kabinda. The northern bank of the
actual mouth fell to the Congo State, which therefore
shared with Portugal the outlet of the Congo. North

of Kabinda came the French Congo, now a great and constantly growing territory, in which the older Gaboon and Ogove dependencies were merged, and which developed into French Equatorial Africa. France and Germany had come to an understanding as to their mutual positions on the western side of Africa before 1885 ended. On the eastern side they could not clash, because France did not come below the Red Sea. On the west the French held all the coast and far into the interior up to the Cameroons, with the exception of the small and still apparently undefined Spanish holding on the Muni river.

When the German flag was hoisted in the Cameroons, the British Government declared Ambas Bay, on which, at Victoria, was the Baptist mission station, to be British and retained it, while otherwise recognizing the German Protectorate in 1885. But the Germans were told that it could be given up, if they could come to terms with the missionaries, and the latter had in effect no option but to consent to be bought out in 1887. It is satisfactory that since the late war this district has come back under mandate to Great Britain. The two Powers agreed that the German Protectorate should end on the coast at the Rio del Rey Creek and from that point up to the Lagos boundary Germany recognized British Protectorate. That Protectorate, now, with Lagos, forming the great Province of Nigeria, began on the coast with what was called at first the Oil Rivers Protectorate and later the Niger Coast Protectorate, and which covered the whole delta of the Niger. Inland the position was saved for Great Britain by treaties with native potentates which had been secured by the National African Company, formed in 1882, and in 1886 given a Royal Charter as the Royal Niger Company, its leading spirit being Sir George Taubman Goldie. All the coast thus became British from the Cameroons to the French Protectorate on the Slave Coast, and inland the British controlled all the lower basin of the Niger and Benue rivers and touched Lake Chad, where all three great Powers, France, Germany, and Great Britain, met.

France was constantly pushing inland from all her footholds on the coast, and also moving down from the north. She had a great ground plan of north and south and west and east expansion, extending behind the British and other foreign possessions, somewhat similar to her ground-plan in North America in the eighteenth century, and the wording of an important Anglo-French Agreement of 1890, whereby the British Government recognized 'the sphere of influence of France to the south of her Mediterranean possessions, up to a line from Say on the Niger to Barruwa on Lake Chad', shows how far she had already by that date carried continuous claims. To appreciate the difference between French and British policy and methods in Africa, reference should be made to a most interesting dispatch of Lord Salisbury, written in March 1892 and published for Parliament in June 1892 (Africa No. 7, 1892). Her general understanding with Germany got rid of some inconvenient German claims on the coast north of the Gulf of Guinea. Her arrangement with Portugal eliminated an old Portuguese claim at Whydah on the Slave Coast, and settled the boundaries of Portuguese Guinea higher up the west coast, leaving her free to expand outside them. In effect she obtained a free hand in her rivalry with Great Britain, with whom there were many treaties and agreements, but no one comprehensive settlement like the Anglo-German Treaty of 1890. On the Gulf of Guinea next to British Lagos and its Protectorate, came the French Slave Coast, now Dahomey, then Togoland, German since 1884, then the British Gold Coast, then the French Ivory Coast, all these dependencies being carried more and more inland by a series of boundary agreements. Farther north came Liberia, then Sierra Leone. Then the French held the coast up to Portuguese Guinea, and north of Portuguese Guinea up to the narrow strip of British Gambia, and then again all the Senegambia region up to Cape Blanco. Here there was a new Protectorate, developed out of old claims, the Spanish Protectorate of the Rio de Oro, notified in 1885, and at first extending to Cape Bojador. Then there was an unappropriated stretch of Sahara coast, on which, at Cape Juby, a British subject in 1879 obtained, and held for a time, a concession, and then came Morocco, still independent, the southern boundary of Morocco being at the time quite indefinite.

*Results and main features of the scramble up to 1891.* Thus, by the end of 1891, in the course of ten years, the partition of Africa among European Powers had in the main been established. The Republic of Liberia was independent, so was Morocco, so virtually was Abyssinia, in spite of the Italian claim to Protectorate over it. Tripoli was still a Turkish province; the Sudan had revolted from Egypt; some of the Sahara coast, and some central regions, had not yet been fully appropriated. In the following period, which will be dealt with in the next chapter, some vital changes will be noticed, and many minor modifications by numberless boundary agreements; but the map of Africa, as it stood in 1914, had in most respects been drawn by 1891. The Powers which before 1880 held African possessions, Spain, Portugal, France, and Great Britain, had all increased their possessions, France and Great Britain very largely. Two new Powers, Germany and Italy, had pegged out very wide claims, the Congo State had brought in Belgians, and eventually Belgium as a nation. This International State was the centre point, the core, of the whole Partition. Its origin followed immediately upon the practical completion of African discovery, and it came into being in the basin of the last of the great African rivers to be traced from source to mouth. The Power which had perhaps the greatest say in the Partition was the newest comer, Germany, fresh from her successful unification in Europe. In spite of the territorial additions which accrued to the British Empire, the Partition was not to the mind of Great Britain, and was in no small degree at the expense of Great Britain, especially on the eastern side of Africa. Germany and France joined hands against her, and Portugal attached herself to these two Powers in preference to her old ally.

The phrase 'Spheres of Influence' came into vogue *Spheres of* in connexion with the scramble for Africa. It repre- *Influence.* sented the first stage, the preparatory stage, of European intrusion. Two Powers competing for footholds in the same region agreed upon some natural boundary, or line of latitude or longitude, on either side of which the one would not interfere with the other. Preserves were, so to speak, marked out in advance of actual Protectorate or annexation. The rights of the Africans in their own lands were practically ignored, and there is nothing to be said in justification, except that what now happened in Africa had happened all over the world from the beginning of time. Everywhere, and at all times, the stronger and more civilized have encroached upon the weaker and more barbarous, and especially the white men upon the coloured men. If it is asked why Great Britain took a hand in the game of grab, the answer is that she did so only because circumstances, contrary to the wishes of her Government, forced her to do so, and, if she had not done so, the natives who were brought under her control would have fared worse in other hands.

*Chartered Companies.* She did so, however, also because, as at other times and in other parts of the world, British traders and missionaries had created British interests in advance of British dominion. Missionaries were very especially pioneers of Empire in Nyasaland and Uganda, and it is not possible to ignore the work of the three great African chartered companies which came into being in these years, the Royal Niger Company, the Imperial British East Africa Company, and the British South Africa Company. There was a new birth of chartered companies at this time, when foreign competition for trade and territory had become accentuated. There is much to be said against chartered companies from the political side. They are formed to make money rather than to rule; the combination of trade and administration is vicious in principle and what it may lead to in practice was horribly illustrated in the Belgian Congo. The case against such combination is summed up admirably by Lord Cromer in his essay on *Ancient and Modern Imperialism.*[1] But the British Empire has been largely the offspring of trade, and the chartered company has been a great factor in the trade and in the Empire which has been founded upon that trade. To a chartered company we owe our Indian Empire, the Hudson Bay Company brought to us the north-west of Canada, and our present position in Africa is

[1] Published by John Murray, 1910. See pp. 69-70.

largely due to chartered companies, although these later companies had not the monopoly of trade which was enjoyed under earlier charters.[1]  While criticizing the obviously weak points of chartered companies, it is impossible to overlook their services in making the British Empire.

181164

[1] The difference between the later type of charter and the older will be found set out in Lord Granville's dispatch to Sir R. Morier of 7th January 1882 with regard to the charter granted in 1881 to the British North Borneo Company (printed in Parliamentary Paper C. 3108, 1882).  The two main points of difference are that in the later charters the Crown assumed no dominion or sovereignty over the territories occupied by the companies under concessions from native potentates, and that a general monopoly of trade was prohibited instead of being granted.

# VI

## THE SCRAMBLE FOR AFRICA, 1891–1914; RAILWAYS

In the story of the Partition of Africa, the period 1891 to 1914 falls into two distinct sections, the dividing line being at the end of 1904. The years 1891 to 1904 were years of war in Africa. Over and above minor expeditions and much local fighting, these years saw the reconquest of the Sudan, the war between Italy and Abyssinia, the South African war, and the prolonged war between the Germans and the Herreros in South-West Africa.

*1891 to 1904.* First let us deal with Egypt and the Sudan. In 1898 the battle of Omdurman and Lord Kitchener's entry into Khartoum completed in the main the recovery of the Sudan, which was placed under joint British and Egyptian control. No place was given to Turkey in the condominium, on grounds explained by Lord Cromer in *Modern Egypt*,[1] that the possession or repossession of the Sudan was achieved by conquest, in which Turkey had no hand, whereas Great Britain as the predominant partner was directly involved. The Fashoda incident is still fresh in the memory. The British arrival at Khartoum coincided with the appearance at Fashoda, higher up the White Nile, of a small French colonial force which, under the command of Major Marchand, had come across from the French Congo. Thus French and British were directly opposed

[1] 1908 ed., vol. ii, pp. 115–19.

on the main Nile. After much friction the outcome was
an Anglo-French agreement, signed in March 1899, by
which the French were finally and definitively excluded
from the Nile basin, the boundary line being drawn
between Wadai on the west and Darfur on the east,
Darfur being left in the British sphere of influence and
Wadai in the French. This agreement barred a farther
west to east expansion by the French. Germany had
already been explicitly barred from extending from the
Cameroons into the Nile basin by an Anglo-German
agreement of 1893 and, except that German East Africa
included half the Victoria Nyanza, which is the ultimate
source of the Nile, and for the leases mentioned in the
last chapter, which gave the Congo State access to the
Nile basin, the whole of that region passed exclusively
under British control. The leases in question, first
granted in 1894 and subsequently modified in 1906,
had been coupled at first with a corresponding lease
from the Congo State to Great Britain of a strip of
territory between lakes Tanganyika and Albert Edward,
secured with a view to giving Great Britain continuous communication between South and North Africa,
and providing a route for the Cape to Cairo railway.
This lease, however, was strongly opposed by Germany
and had to be dropped. Thus the different Powers
barred one another's progress. Portugal, as we have
seen, tried to make good a claim to a transcontinental
belt, which would have cut across British northward
expansion, but which in the event Great Britain cut
through. Great Britain barred French eastward extension to the Nile, and Germany barred British continuity from south to north. We shall come later to
one more illustration of this sort of thing. Meanwhile,
to return to Egypt and the Sudan, the exact boundaries

on the eastern side with Italian Eritrea were settled by a series of agreements.

*Abys-sinia.*      It has been said that the Italians had asserted a kind of Protectorate over Abyssinia. Italy claimed that, by a treaty of 1889, the Abyssinians had placed their foreign relations in her hands, a claim which was tantamount to a Protectorate. Some years later Italy and Abyssinia came to blows, the Italians were heavily defeated at Adowa in 1896, and signed a treaty in that year, which recognized the independence of Abyssinia. This put an end to the ambitious Italian scheme for linking up inland Eritrea on the Red Sea with Italian Somaliland on the Indian Ocean. There followed a series of treaties defining the Italian, French, and British boundaries with Abyssinia and—to look beyond 1904— in 1906 these three Powers jointly guaranteed Abyssinian independence.

*East, South, and West Africa.*      On the eastern side of Africa, as indeed in Africa generally, these years were years of consolidating claims, and of defining and usually modifying the inland boundaries, which became more difficult as they were carried farther inland and as they were discovered to be in conflict with geographical facts. In the British sphere in East Africa the Imperial British East Africa Company came to an end, British East Africa and Uganda became Protectorates directly under the British Crown, and what was known as the Uganda Railway was constructed from Mombasa to the Victoria Lake. In South Africa Great Britain carried her control of the east coast right up to the Portuguese boundary and inland the Boer republics disappeared, as a result of the South African War. On the western side, Spanish Guinea or Muni became defined by a Franco-Spanish Convention of 1900, whereby France and

Spain came to an understanding both as to Spanish
Guinea and as to the more northern Spanish Protectorate
of the Rio de Oro; France secured the right of
pre-emption in both places.  Northward from and including the Cameroons, the boundary questions became
peculiarly difficult of adjustment, and the boundary
conventions were many.  It was in the Niger regions
and the Gulf of Guinea that the three great Powers,
Germany, France, and Great Britain, all three converging in Lake Chad, met and collided most.  The
configuration of Africa in the Gulf of Guinea added
to the difficulty.  The boundary lines had to be drawn
both north and south and east and west.  The Power
that gained most in actual territory was undoubtedly
France.  She consolidated her coast-line.  On the Slave
Coast she conquered and absorbed Dahomey.  On the
Ivory Coast she finally closed up all the gap between
the Gold Coast and Liberia.  On all her sections of
the coast she pressed inland and at the same time came
down from the north.  Thus she secured complete
control of the Upper and Middle Niger, more and
more hemming in the other Powers, especially the
British, and carried her immense Empire continuously
behind Lake Chad from the Mediterranean to the
Congo.

French bitterness against Great Britain culminated at *The
Anglo-
French
Con-
vention of
1904.*
Fashoda and was abundantly shown at the time of the
South African War, which followed shortly afterwards.
When that war had ended, when King Edward with his
warm sympathy for France had succeeded to Queen
Victoria, and while Lord Lansdowne was at the Foreign
Office in London, the relations between the two Powers
began to improve, and eventually, in 1904, the long
misunderstanding was laid to rest.  On the 8th of April,

1904, a treaty or convention was signed, sometimes known as the Newfoundland Treaty, because Newfoundland figured as prominently in it as Heligoland in the Anglo-German Treaty of 1890. Great Britain gained outside Africa and lost territory in Africa. In return for the surrender of French privileges on the Newfoundland coast, France was given ground on the Gambia and in Nigeria and received the group of small islands known as the Isles de Los, which had been in British possession since 1818 and formed part of the colony of Sierra Leone, though lying to the north of it and over against Konakry in French West Africa. On the same day an equally important joint declaration or agreement was signed whereby Great Britain agreed not to obstruct France in Morocco, and France agreed not to obstruct Great Britain in Egypt. Secret articles, which were made public in 1911, committed each country still further. France and Spain, in the same year, also made a joint declaration as to Morocco and added secret articles, communicated to Great Britain at the time and made public in 1911, which defined the Spanish zones and determined Franco-Spanish relations in Morocco. The published declarations did not infringe the independence of Morocco, but the Secret Articles provided for conditions under which Morocco might not remain independent, and in a contingency France and Spain were assured of the support of Great Britain. The vital importance of the 1904 agreements between France and Great Britain was that the estrangement between these two Powers, which had so successfully furthered German designs in Africa, now disappeared, and after 1904 Germany, not Great Britain, suffered isolation. This was, for Germany, a hard fact both to realize and to accept, and it is impossible to resist the conclusion that the clash of European interests in Africa, and the feeling which they called forth, were among the determining causes of the war of 1914.

In 1904 Morocco was the most important part of *1904 to* Africa which had not so far been parcelled out.   It was *1914.* in Africa what Turkey was in Europe—the 'sick man' among the states.   Like Egypt before the British inter-vened, Morocco fermented with anarchy.   As British intervention in Egypt was a kind of prelude to the first stage of the scramble for Africa, and as the resentment of France against Great Britain caused by that inter-vention was a leading factor in shaping the subsequent partition, so the beginning of the last stage in the scramble was marked by German attempts to intervene in Morocco, resulting in strained relations between France and Germany.   In the first stage France had, more or less, the backing of Germany.   In the last stage she enjoyed in a much greater degree the backing of Great Britain.   The French made proposals to Morocco *Morocco.* for reforms; while they were being considered the Kaiser visited Tangier at the end of March 1905, the Sultan refused the French proposals and, no doubt at German instigation, suggested a conference of the Powers, which Germany at once accepted.   The position taken up by Germany was intelligible; she had not been a party to the Anglo-French agreement, she had interests in Morocco, and was concerned to maintain the inde-pendence of Morocco.   The general view of the other Powers was that France, the immediate neighbour of Morocco and the Power most closely concerned in Morocco, should determine whether or no a conference was advisable.   Great Britain, in particular, would not accept a conference unless and until France accepted. The Germans became aggressive to France, German backstairs influence led to the resignation of M. Delcassé, the French Foreign Minister, and eventually France, on assurance from Germany that French rights in Morocco, so far as they were consistent with the independence of Morocco, would not be compromised, agreed to the conference, which was held at Algeciras in January 1906. In April 1906 a general act of the conference was signed, which embodied or professed to embody reforms based upon the independence and integrity of Morocco and on economic liberty and equality in Morocco for all the Powers. But, contrary to the strong wish of Germany and as a result of the backing given to France by Great Britain, Russia and Italy, France and Spain— in certain points connected with the police and the enforcement of regulations—were given preference as being specially concerned. The Act was duly accepted by the Sultan. It will be noticed that, just as Germany promoted the Berlin Conference in 1884, so she promoted the Algeciras Conference ; and, as the Berlin Conference was a sort of counterblast to the stillborn Congo Treaty between Great Britain and Portugal, so the Algeciras Conference was a retort to the Anglo-French Treaty of 1904. In other words, international machinery was on both occasions invoked to checkmate a treaty between two Powers which did not suit the purposes and interests of other Powers.

The internal condition of Morocco did not improve. In 1907 the French again intervened, sending a cruiser to the port of Casablanca on the Atlantic coast and fighting on the Algerian border. In the same year France, Spain, and Great Britain exchanged notes agreeing to stand together. In 1908 civil war deposed the Sultan of Morocco and brought his half-brother to the throne, and there was again dangerous friction

between France and Germany caused by an incident
at Casablanca, where deserters from the French Foreign
Legion, of German nationality, took refuge at the German consulate but were recaptured by the French
police. In 1909 the two Powers came to a friendly
understanding as to their respective rights in Morocco,
and in 1910 the country seemed to be settling down.
But in 1911 there was civil war again, both French and
Spanish troops marched into Morocco, and the Germans
thereupon sent a gunboat to the Atlantic port of Agadir,
nominally to protect German interests, really to threaten
intervention. Eventually, in November 1911, France
and Germany settled their differences by three agreements (one called an Exchange of Notes). Germany gave *The
Franco-
German
Agree-
ment of
1911.*
France a free hand in Morocco, and France ceded to
Germany a net 100,000 square miles of the French
Congo, which were added to the eastern or southern
side of the Cameroons. It will be well first to follow
out what happened in Morocco and then to look at the
enlarged Cameroons.

In 1912 the Sultan of Morocco signed a treaty accept- *France
and Spain
in
Morocco.*
ing a French Protectorate, and later in the year France
and Spain signed a new treaty which, read with the
1904 agreement, defined the respective zones and
interests of the two Powers in and near Morocco. It is
very difficult to understand the exact details of the
settlement and to harmonize the wording of the Franco-
Spanish and Franco-German agreements, but the result
seems to have been as follows. On the Atlantic coast
the southern boundary of Morocco was placed at 27·40
of north latitude, and the Spanish dependency of the
Rio de Oro, which came to be referred to as a colony,
and of which the French had the pre-emption, was
extended up to that point. The coast between 27·40

and the Wad Draa river, formerly known as the Nun, was spoken of as in Southern Morocco, but up to the Wad Draa France gave Spain a free hand to establish herself. Thus all the Atlantic coast from Cape Blanco north to the Wad Draa was left to Spain, whose colony of the Canary Islands lay over against the northern section of this coast. The Wad Draa, which is in about 28·42 north latitude, is geographically the dividing line between the Sahara and Morocco, and here the French Protectorate began. But within Morocco, as it was bounded on the south by the Wad Draa, there were two Spanish zones and one international zone. The main Spanish zone included the old Spanish possessions of Ceuta, Melilla, and their surroundings. It covered, within a line drawn inland according to the treaties, the Mediterranean coast of Morocco from the mouth of the Wad Mulaya, south-east of Melilla, westward to the neighbourhood of Tangier, and, on the other side of Tangier, the Atlantic coast down to the 35th parallel of north latitude, just below Larache. Farther south on the Atlantic coast in the south-west of Morocco was another very small Spanish zone, known as the Ifni enclave, which originated in a cession of ground for a fishing establishment, made by Morocco to Spain in 1860. In addition to these two Spanish zones in Morocco, Tangier with its vicinity was constituted, somewhat indefinitely, an international zone. Elsewhere in Morocco a French Protectorate is in force.

*Exten-sion of the Came-roons.* The price which France paid to Germany for German concession in regard to Morocco was a great slice of the French Congo or Equatorial Africa, which was added to the German Cameroons. In this region Germany ceded to France 7,000 square miles, and France to Germany 107,000 square miles. From the main mass of territory thus given to Germany three tongues of land protruded, of much political importance. The first, a very narrow strip, ran due east and west along the southern border of the Spanish Protectorate, giving Germany access to the sea south of that Protectorate, and making it an enclave in German territory. At the same time the pre-emption of the Spanish quadrilateral, which France had held, was transferred to Germany. The second, running nearly due south down the Sanga river, which is a tributary of the Congo, gave the Germans that river and brought them down to the main Congo, planting them on it directly over against the Belgian Congo. The third, which was farther north, and which ran to the south-east, brought the Germans on to the Ubangi river, another affluent of the Congo. The result was to give the Germans access to the Congo (just as by the Anglo-German Treaty of 1890 and the Caprivi Strip they had gained access to the Zambesi), to place them opposite to the Belgian Congo on the Congo, as they were opposite to it on Lake Tanganyika, and to cut the continuity of the French Congo with French Central Africa, though the French still held the water communication and kept the islands in the rivers which they owned before 1911. In short, Germany gave up all prospect of any territorial foothold in North Africa, but very greatly strengthened her position in Central Africa.

There was one more change in the map of Africa of *Italian occupation of Tripoli.* first-rate importance. In 1911, shortly before France and Germany came to terms, Italy found occasion to go to war with Turkey and invaded Tripoli. It has been seen that Italy had greatly resented the French Protectorate of Tunis, and later she had reason to suspect German designs on Tripoli. If Tripoli were to pass into the hands of another Power, there would be no place left for Italy in North Africa, and consequently she took action.  By the treaty of Lausanne in October 1912, which ended the war, she wrested from Turkey the sovereignty of Tripoli and Cyrenaica.  This completed the partition of Africa as it stood in 1914, Liberia and Abyssinia being the only unallotted parts.

*Main fea-*
*tures of*
*the Parti-*
*tion and*
*respective*
*positions*
*of the*
*Powers.*

It will be well to sum up the main features of this partition and note how the Powers stood in Africa in 1914.  The North Coast, with the exception of Egypt, where Great Britain was dominant, was given to the three Latin and Mediterranean Powers, France, Spain, and Italy, France being incomparably in the strongest position of the three.  In North-East Africa, France, Italy, and Great Britain alone were concerned.  The southernmost limit of Italy in Africa was the Juba river.  The southernmost limit of France on the eastern side of the mainland was Tajoura, and here was the only French possession on this side of the continent; but, in the course of the partition, the French had finally secured control of the great island of Madagascar.  Below the Juba river came Great Britain, Germany, Portugal, and Great Britain again.  The southern end of Africa was wholly British—on the western side only as far as the Orange river.  Inland Great Britain held an immense and continuous stretch of territory from the Cape up to the region of the Great Lakes, reaching beyond the Zambesi to Lakes Nyasa and Tanganyika.  On the west side from the Orange river to the mouth of the Congo came Germany and then Portugal.  The Congo State just touched the sea on the north bank of the mouth of the Congo, then came the little isolated Portuguese section of Kabinda, and then the French began, this being the southernmost limit of the French on the mainland; thus, while the French were predominant in North Africa, they had no *locus standi* whatever in South Africa. From this point, upwards and inwards, France, Germany, and Great Britain were in and out of each other's territory for a long way. Still, as in the old slaving days, the Guinea regions were the great meeting-place of Europeans. The German land farthest north in Africa was Togoland, so that in all the great northern half of the continent Germany had no place. On the western side north of Togoland, with the exception of Liberia and small Portuguese Guinea, France and Great Britain alone were concerned, up to and including the Gambia. There British influence ceased, and the field was left to France and Spain.

Of the three greatest Powers, Germany, France, and Great Britain, France had the largest and widest continuous area of empire. Germany had four dependencies in Africa, all detached from each other, and in all she was side by side with Great Britain. This illustrates what was said in the last chapter, that, if the partition *The posi-* in its early stages could be said to have been at the *tion of* *Germany* expense of any one of the European Powers already in *in Africa.* Africa, it was at the expense of Great Britain. It was in regions where British interests were more especially involved that Germany established herself. Though the German dependencies were not continuous, yet, at the end of the partition, Germany held, perhaps, the best strategic position of all the Powers. Her main African possession was German East Africa. It abutted on all the three great African lakes, Victoria, Tanganyika, and Nyasa, and she held the whole eastern side of the centremost lake, Tanganyika, where she fronted the Belgian Congo, while her latest deal with France in the Cameroons brought her on to the Congo, again

over against the Belgian Congo at another point. As
has been pointed out, and as the map shows, the
Belgian Congo is the core of Africa, and in 1914
Germany was in a very strong position for striking
at it. The intense opposition, which she successfully
offered to the lease which would have given Great
Britain a right of way through the Congo, showed that
she did not intend her position to be in any way
menaced or weakened. South-West Africa gave her
a foothold on the flank of the British in South Africa
and, as was shown when the War came, an opportunity
for supporting any Dutch movement against British
supremacy. The Caprivi Strip brought her on to the
Zambesi. In the Cameroons she gained access to the
Congo in one direction, in another to Lake Chad, and,
so far as she controlled the upper waters of the Benue,
to the Niger basin. She had in short a ground plan
for a Central African Empire, and no doubt, when she
decided to leave North Africa to others, she looked to
achieving such an empire all the more.

*France and Great Britain.* Turning to the positions held by France and Great
Britain respectively, let us see how they stood on the
African waterways. France controlled the Senegal
wholly, the Gambia in part, the Upper and Middle
Niger wholly, with a privileged footing on the Lower
Niger held by leases from Great Britain granted in
1898. She was in strength on the Congo. On the
other hand, she had no lot or part on the Nile or the
Zambesi, or on any of the Great Lakes, except Lake
Chad. Great Britain controlled the Lower Gambia, the
Lower Niger, the Nile wholly, the Zambesi partially.
She had nothing to do with the Congo except at its
extreme headwaters. She had a footing on all the lakes,
but only held the southernmost end of Lake Tanganyika.

She was the only Power which was in evidence in all parts of Africa, except the North-West, and close to the North-West she held Gibraltar over against Ceuta and Tangier.

Before the war various European dependencies in *Enclaves in Africa.* Africa were entirely encircled by other European Powers. All the four Spanish dependencies were enclaves of this kind. Spanish Guinea was encircled by Germany, and the Rio de Oro and the Spanish zones in Morocco by France. France encircled Portuguese Guinea and the British Gambia. German South-West Africa encircled Walfish Bay. In no case did Great Britain encircle another European dependency.

As the partition went on railways became more and *Railways in Africa.* more important. The Beira Railway figures in the Anglo-Portuguese Treaty of 1891, and railways enter into other and later International Agreements. In some parts of the world railways have surmounted or burrowed under mountain barriers, the Alps, for instance, or the Rocky Mountains. Africa is not rich in definitive mountain ranges serving as political barriers. The Atlas range in the far North-West, and the Drakensberg in the far South-East, are perhaps the most noteworthy, and the railway from Durban makes its way through the Drakensberg to the Orange Free State Province and the Transvaal. There is, however, a more or less steep ascent from the coast to the inland plateau in South and Central Africa, and railway communication has been of the utmost value in surmounting this ascent.[1] A sharp ascent means falls and rapids in the rivers. We have seen, on the one hand, that the African rivers are

---

[1] For the immense value of railways to South Africa, see Lord Milner's Address on 'Geography and Statecraft' in *The Nation and the Empire* (Constable, 1913).

most disappointing as highways, and, on the other hand, that the opening up of Africa turned on the opening up of waterways. What bearing then have railways had upon the waterways of Africa? In the first place, they have obviously made, or begun to make, the waterways of less importance. Before the days of railways, rivers and lakes, even when very defective, were used to the utmost. Railways tend to supersede them, just as flying bids fair at some future date to supersede both waterways and railways. In the second place, railways in Africa have served very specially in making good the defects of the rivers. They have here and there been constructed to make portages past non-navigable parts of the rivers, as on the Senegal, the Congo, and the Nile. In the case of the Nile, at its very beginning, there is a short railway which makes a portage past the outlet of the river from Lake Victoria by the Ripon Falls; and the Wadi Halfa–Khartoum Railway gets round cataracts and also cuts off a great semicircle of the river. In the third place, they have a special value in Africa in linking up the inland seas, the Great Lakes, with the outer ocean, as in the case of the Uganda railway to Lake Victoria and the Central Railway in what was German East Africa to Lake Tanganyika. A good instance of railways being constructed or designed to make good defective waterways and to link up the Great Lakes with the ocean is to be found in Nyasaland. The Shiré River in some sort connects Lake Nyasa with the Zambesi, and therefore with the sea, but the river in the neighbourhood of the Shiré Highlands is useless for navigation, it is of little use between the Highlands and the Lake, and throughout its whole course it is becoming more and more useless owing to the fall in the level of Lake Nyasa. A railway has been constructed from Blantyre in the Highlands to Chindio on the Zambesi and, in the other direction, it is intended to be carried from Blantyre to the end of the lake. But the Zambesi again is very bad for navigation, especially at the mouth, where, at Chinde, the Portuguese have leased to Great Britain [1] a landing-place, as mentioned in an Annexe to the Anglo-Portuguese Treaty of 1891. Consequently it is proposed to bridge the Zambesi and carry the railway down to Beira. Similarly, the Lukuga, the one river outlet from Lake Tanganyika, flowing to the Congo, is useless as a waterway from the lake, and a Belgian railway has been constructed along its course to the Upper Congo.

The English, and especially Cecil Rhodes, must be credited with taking the lead in railway construction in Africa. In 1897 the great northward line from Cape Town reached Buluwayo, a distance of 1,360 miles. In 1902 this line was linked to the east coast at Beira. It was carried north across the Zambesi at the Victoria Falls; in 1909 it reached the frontier of the Congo State, and during the late war through railway communication was completed for 2,600 miles from Capetown to the navigable Congo at Bukama. In Nigeria, in 1911, a railway was completed for 700 miles inland from Lagos to Kano. The line from Wadi Halfa to Khartoum, 578 miles long, was completed in 1899, and the line from Atbara junction on this Khartoum Railway to Port Sudan on the Red Sea in 1906; this last is of great political importance because it gives to the Sudan an outlet to the sea other than the outlet through Egypt. By 1902 the Uganda Railway,

---

[1] This lease is not on all fours with other international leases, e.g. the leases to the French on the Niger. It is in form a lease not to Great Britain or the British Government, but to a personal representative of Great Britain.

582 miles long, had been finished, linking up Lake
Victoria to the Indian Ocean. Of non-British railways
the most important completed work before the war was
the German trunk line in East Africa from Dâr-es-
Salaam to Tanganyika, nearly 800 miles long, which
was completed and opened early in 1914. The French
were very active in railway building in Senegambia and
in the basin of the Upper Niger, but a French writer in
1916 estimated that, between 1908 and 1913, French
railways in Africa had increased only by 21 per cent. as
against over a 100 per cent. increase in German railways.
The French, however, have long had far-reaching
schemes of railway development, and among other lines,
a French railway was in 1915 completed from the Red
Sea coast to the centre of Abyssinia, an example of a
railway climbing into a mountain zone. In Portuguese
West Africa there is at Lobito Bay, the sea terminus of
an important line, the Benguela Railway, which has
been constructed for over 300 miles and which will give
a westward outlet to the Katanga district of the Belgian
Congo, now dependent on the Cape to Cairo Railway.
In short, at all points railways are running inland from
the coast, and everywhere on the waterways small
sections of railway are making good the defects in water
communication. For good or for evil the Dark Continent
has been brought to light.

# VII

## NORTH AFRICA

M. JULES CAMBON, who was Governor-General of <comment-marginal>European intrusion into other continents.</comment-marginal>Algeria between 1891 and 1897, spoke of Algeria as being at once a *colonie de peuplement* and a *colonie d'exploitation.* As is well known, European intrusion into other continents has been either a matter of *peuplement*—of peopling and settlement, or a matter of *exploitation,* of making money out of the lands and out of the peoples by plantations, trade, and generally by what is euphemistically called 'peaceful penetration'; occasionally it has been a matter of both, as M. Cambon says has been the case in Algeria. It must be repeated that the justification for intrusion of either kind can only be found in the instinct of the human race from the beginning of time, and such intrusion seems to be inseparable from human progress.

Among the continents, Asia and Europe have been mutual intruders, Asia apparently having been the first offender, if it is an offence to have been, as we are told, the original home of migrating humanity. Modern history has been mainly a story of European intrusion, which, as in Australasia, resents subsequent Asiatic intrusion. Setting then Europe in one category, as the aggressor, and all the other continents in another, as the victims of aggression, it is obvious that climate in the first place, and the kind of native races in the second have, in the main, determined whether the aggression has taken the form of peopling or of exploiting. In America and Australasia it has been more especially a matter of peopling, of settlement, because in those continents are very large areas in temperate climates, with comparatively small numbers of native inhabitants, and these lacking in stamina. It is a wholly different matter if we turn to Asia. Northern Asia—Siberia—has been Europeanized, or at any rate Russianized, but tropical Asia could not be and has not been; and not only in tropical Asia, but in China, for instance, and Japan, both thickly populated by very strong races, there has not been and there could not be any possibility of the substitution of white for native races. European intrusion into Asia, therefore, in the main, has been of the nature of exploiting.

Africa presents some special features of European intrusion. In the first place, it should be remembered that Africa was in two sections at the dawn of modern history, and that North and North-East Africa should be classed with the Old World, and the rest of Africa with the New Worlds—as a field of exploration and discovery the newest of the New Worlds. In the second place, Africa, the most tropical of the continents, and peopled by very strong and reproductive native races, is peculiarly a field of exploitation more than of settlement. It is nowhere a field for unchallenged European *peuplement* —for settlement in the sense of exclusive European colonization, that is of substituting a white immigrant for a coloured native population. The areas suited for European settlement are also the homes of native races, which show no signs whatever of decay, and consequently these are most difficult areas where European intrusion takes shape both as *peuplement* and as *exploitation*. It is the presence of a native population far outnumbering the whites, and increasing in greater proportion than the whites, which gives to the Union of South Africa a wholly different character from the other Self-Governing Dominions.

These areas are, with exceptions, such as the High- *North* lands of East Africa and the plateau of Southern *and South Africa* Rhodesia, both of which are in the tropics, regions *com-* in the temperate but subtropical zones. The southern- *pared.* most end is nearer to the tropic line than the north-westernmost. In South Africa the desert is on the western side. In North Africa it is on the southern, and also, between Tripoli and Egypt, on the eastern side. In other words, the continuity of Africa is much more broken by desert in the north than it is in the south. Though the southernmost end is nearer the tropics than the north-western, the climate of South Africa is more favourable to colonization by the races of Northern Europe than is North Africa. Presumably, North Africa, lying between an enclosed sea and the Sahara, concentrates heat more than the southern peninsula, with the open ocean on the low-lying coast-lines, and with high plateaux inland. At any rate the Mediterranean seaboard suits the Latin races of Mediterranean Europe, and South Africa suits the Dutch and British, the only Latin element in South Africa, other than French missionaries, being the very interesting Huguenot element among the Boers. North-West Africa, including Morocco, Algeria, and Tunis, is in effect very much of an island, and is in the main a French sphere, as South Africa is a British sphere, both being regions where Europeans have made homes side by side with native Africans and also Asiatic immigrants. Taking the most developed part of either region, in Algeria, in 1911, the Europeans were estimated as one in six, in the Union of South Africa rather over one in five. In the

Union the Dutch were established prior to the British, and are more numerous than the British. In Algeria there are many Europeans besides French. In 1895, for instance, M. Cambon spoke of 260,000 French and 250,000 other Europeans. In 1911, according to the *Statesman's Year Book*, the French numbered 492,000, and, among other Europeans, the Spaniards numbered 135,000, but there is no European race which has competed with the French in Algeria to the same extent as that to which the Dutch preceded and compete with the British in South Africa.

*North Africa.* Now, although North and South Africa are alike in being African regions where Europeans have not only exploited but settled, yet there are endless differences between the two spheres, and of these differences two are obvious and outstanding. North Africa is close to, South Africa removed from, Europe ; and North Africa is an orientalized Africa, while South Africa, though large numbers of East Indians and some Malays have been brought in, is essentially a land of the African.

*Effect of the nearness of North Africa to Europe.* What effect has the nearness of North Africa to Europe had on modern European intrusion into Africa? In the first place, it has given historical justification for the intrusion. It can be regarded, as Freeman regarded it,[1] as a process of winning back what had been an outskirt of Europe (and, after the Christian era, of Christian Europe), of recovering land which had been taken from Europe not by Africa but by Asia; and certainly, if we look for worthy heirs of the old Roman Empire, the French, as has been already suggested, have much of the Roman type in them. This is perhaps rather a fanciful point, a second and much more practical

[1] See above, p. 23.

consideration is that when North Africa harboured a
race of pirates, mere proximity made it such a nuisance
to Europe as not merely to provide an excuse for
European intrusion, but almost to make it a necessity.
Armed intervention in Algeria followed by conquest
was the outcome of perpetual provocation by Algerian
pirates. The French occupied Algiers by force of
arms in 1830, very much as, at a later date, in 1882,
the British occupied Egypt, the occupation being due,
in the first instance, to force of circumstances, rather
than design of permanent conquest and annexation.
Then there followed long years of war, Algeria became
a conquered territory, and the piracy, which had pro-
voked the intervention, disappeared. In the third
place, the nearness of Europe had, even under the
old conditions, brought a European, or at any rate
a cosmopolitan element, into North Africa. The number
of Christians carried off by the pirates was very considerable, and many of them must have been absorbed
in the population. Some of the most noted leaders
among the corsairs were European Christians, who
had turned into Mussulmen. There is a large number
of Jews in North Africa, recruited, no doubt, after the
expulsion of the Jews from Spain. Like the Spanish
Moors, many of the Spanish Jews probably found an
asylum in Africa. Europe's excuse then for intruding
into North Africa was that North Africa had been a
European possession; that it was aggressive and pro-
vocative at the doors of Europe; and that, in one way
or another, European elements had filtered into it. In
a word North Africa was, and could not help being,
a concern of Europe, and latter-day European intrusion
followed as a consequence both of its history and of its
geography.

*Effect of the orientalizing of North Africa.*  Now comes the second feature, that it was an Eastern and Mohammedan sphere, which had supplanted a European régime. It did not present itself to modern European intrusion as a scene of virgin barbarism, but rather as the home of decayed communities and states of the Eastern and Moslem type, and decay, in communities as in plants, invites new life—alien and often parasitic. Europeans gained a financial footing, and money claims led on to political control. So it was in Tunis, in Morocco, in Egypt. It is the oriental character of North Africa which has mainly decided the lines which European intervention has followed. It has been such intrusion as is familiar in Eastern countries, originating with concessions, loans and so forth, representatives or private citizens of rival European nations besetting some weak and embarrassed native potentate with rival claims, and eventually one or another of these nations becoming masters of the field. North Africa was in short not a primitive African Africa, but an Asiatic Africa run to seed; its unsettled political life invited exploitation, and exploitation followed.

*The French in Algeria.*  Algeria, however, the first large modern European acquisition in North Africa, is another story. It was acquired before North Africa was ripe for exploiting and before the full tide of modern exploiting had set in. It was not gained by a preliminary process of financial intrigue, but by plain conquest. No one can doubt that it has gained immensely by coming under French rule and by the substitution of law and order for anarchy, but it has been a possession both of extraordinary difficulty and of extraordinary interest, and the difficulty has been in no small degree due to its nearness to France. Freeman wrote of it in 1882 as 'a land which in some sort answers alike to India and to Australia, but which lies within two days' sail of her (France's) coast'.[1] By answering alike to India and to Australia is presumably meant that it is (repeating M. Cambon's words), a field both for *exploitation* and for *peuplement*. M. Cambon also laid stress on the point that Algeria is an Eastern country, adding that the coexistence of different races side by side without mixing is characteristic of the East. This feature seems hardly to be peculiar to the East, and it might be argued that non-intermixture arises from difference of religion at least as much as from that of race, the barrier between Mohammedanism, the great Eastern religion, and Christianity being peculiarly strong. M. Cambon drew a clear distinction between Algeria on the one hand and Tunis and Morocco on the other, in that Algeria, he said, never had any appearance either of unity or of monarchy. There was a nominal head, the Dey of Algiers, when the French entered in, but apparently there was less vestige of a State and less semblance of a government than in Morocco on the one side or Tunis on the other. At any rate here the French secured a country which could be colonized as well as exploited, and which was a larger field for French colonization, than any other which France had at the time or still has within her Empire, for, with the loss of Canada, the French were deprived of their main area of *peuplement* overseas. This new field of colonization, being close to France, was most accessible for French colonists, but at the same time it was the home of native races strong with the strength of the unchanging East.

[1] *Hist. Geog. of Europe*, ut sup., p. 373.

In our own Empire we have been fortunate in having had to deal almost entirely with distant provinces. Ireland shows that, when a territory lies at our immediate door, we fumble with the problem, undecided, as it were, between assimilation and autonomy. Algeria was similarly the scene of conflicting views and policies. There was necessarily in the fighting times military administration, and there were attempts at military colonization. After Abd El-Kader had surrendered in 1847, the view was taken that the territory should be colonized from and assimilated to France. As Frenchmen multiplied in the land, they chafed against military rule and, as a safeguard against it, favoured government direct from Paris. This was attempted in 1858, the Governor-General in Algeria was abolished, the administrative head-quarters were removed to Paris, and a ministry of Algeria was created. But in 1860 they went back to a Governor-General. Subsequently Napoleon the Third took a wholly different view to that of assimilation to France, and wrote a letter hinting at an Arab kingdom in Algeria under France. After the Franco-German War the assimilation policy again prevailed, and French colonists multiplied, natives of Alsace-Lorraine, who wished to remain French citizens, were given lands, and vine-growers from the South of France came in. In 1881, though the Governor-General was not abolished, by what were called decrees of *rattachement* the administration was centred in Paris. Ten years later there was a reaction against this extreme centralization, a commission under the chairmanship of Jules Ferry was appointed to consider reforms, M. Jules Cambon was appointed Governor-General, and by the time that he left, in 1897, the decentralizing policy had triumphed, and the Governor-General had regained full powers.

But what has been said applies only to administration. The legislative power over Algeria has always rested with the French Parliament. The great difference between French and British handling of overseas colonies and dependencies seems to be that the French centralize more than the British, and are more inclined to uniformity. The British believe in having the laws made as far as possible where their administration is carried out—on the spot ; they favour local legislatures, varying from nominated Legislative Councils to the fully responsible Parliaments of the Self-Governing Dominions, and they are content with endless diversities, as the localities are diverse. The French find the safeguard for their colonies in giving them in various cases representation in the French Parliament, a step which we have often talked of but never taken. At the present day Algeria, or rather Northern Algeria, is treated as part of France, and has representatives in both the French chambers, having three senators and six deputies, elected practically by the non-Mohammedan population. There is, however, a separate Algerian budget, which is prepared by the Governor-General under the Ministry of the Interior, that is the Home Office. In Algeria the Governor-General is advised by a Council of Government consisting wholly of officials and apparently analogous to the Executive Council in a British colony, and there is a Superior Council and Financial Delegations, on both of which there is an elective element, and on both of which the Mahommedan population is represented. The Superior Council discusses administrative and financial matters, the Delegations deal with taxation and vote the budget.

Thus, while there is no legislative power on the spot, there seems to be some financial control, which in British history has proved the most important of all control in the long run. This applies only to Northern Algeria, and even there apparently some areas are still under military rule. Southern Algeria is a separate colony, in a less advanced stage of organization.

*Tunis and Morocco.* In Tunis, over which the Turks for some time continued to assert claims against the French, and in Morocco, the French appear to have taken very much the same line as so often commends itself to us. They govern through the native rulers, having French Resident Generals, who are not under the Home Office in Paris but under the Foreign Office. Among Europeans in Tunis the Italians apparently outnumber the French, showing that there was some substantial ground for Italian resentment, when France forestalled Italy in Tunis, but accounts seem to agree that the French have been most successful in their administration of Tunis, just as in Morocco they are proving their capacity. Sir Harry Johnston, in his article on Tunis in the last edition (1910–11) of the *Encyclopædia Britannica*, writes: 'The native dynasty has been strengthened rather than weakened, and Tunisia may be pointed out as the best and wisest example of French administration over an alien land and race.' Lord Cromer in *Modern Egypt* points out how much the French were helped in Tunis by Great Britain and other Powers giving up the special privileges which their subjects enjoyed there under the Capitulations, and he also points out,[1] with special reference to Egypt, how much more attractive French civilization is to Orientals and Levantines than British, and French

[1] Vol. ii, 1908 ed., pp. 236–42.

administration too, because it prescribes rules for everything, while the English leave much to individual responsibility. However, France has done much for North Africa, and in turn North Africa has done not a little for France. Algeria has been a school for great French soldiers and administrators, as India has been for us, as well as furnishing an ample supply of good fighting troops.

Italy only acquired Tripoli two years before the war, *Tripoli.* and as both Italy and Turkey, the former owner of Tripoli, were involved in the war on opposite sides, it is too soon to look for the fruits of Italian occupation. This was the only part of Africa which, in 1911, was directly under Turkish rule. Tripoli had become, like Algeria and Tunis, a practically independent pirate State, but in 1835 the Turks reconquered it, and latterly there had been two Turkish provinces, Tripoli and Barca, Barca being the ancient Cyrenaica. Caravan routes lead from Tripoli into the heart of Central Africa. Hence, as we have seen, various exploring expeditions in the early part of the nineteenth century started from Tripoli. From Cyrenaica Mrs. Forbes started on her recent journey to the Senussi head-quarters in the Libyan desert.[1]

While Tripoli, up to 1911, was directly under Turkish *Egypt.* rule, Egypt before the war was an autonomous vassal State of the Ottoman Empire. It paid a tribute to Turkey of £682,000 per annum, which was practically mortgaged to the Ottoman bondholders; the Egyptians were, strictly speaking, Ottoman subjects; in political treaties with Foreign Powers the Turkish Government claimed to speak for Egypt; a maximum of 18,000 men was fixed for the number of the Egyptian Army; and in

[1] See her book *The Secret of the Sahara-Kufara* (Cassell & Co., 1921).

general Turkey had a recognized sovereignty in
Egypt, over and above the reverence attaching to the
Turkish Sultan as Khalif, or spiritual head of the
Mohammedans.   The immediate ruler of Egypt was
styled Khedive, or prince, not Sultan.   On the other
hand, the throne had been made hereditary in the
ruling dynasty, and moreover descended not according to Turkish custom, but by the European
law of primogeniture.   In the main the Khedive
acted independently of the Sultan, and attempts
made by Turkey during the British occupation to
encroach upon Egyptian territory were brought to
nothing.   Modern Egypt was created from Europe, but
from Turkish Europe.   It was the creation, in the earlier
part of the nineteenth century, of the great Albanian
soldier, Mehemet Ali, who was born in the same year as
Napoleon.   At one time his forces, directed against the
Turks, conquered Palestine and Asia Minor, and, if the
European Powers had not intervened, would have made
him master of Constantinople.   Egypt under him was
once more a competitor for an Asiatic Empire, but did
not achieve it.   Mehemet remained a vassal of the
Sultan, though confirmed in his position in Egypt.   We
are fortunate in having the highest authorities for the
record of modern Egypt, especially Lord Milner's
*England in Egypt,* the first edition of which appeared
nearly thirty years ago, Lord Cromer's great book
entitled *Modern Egypt,* and among most recent books
*The Egyptian Problem,* by Sir Valentine Chirol.

Egypt, although 'the land of paradox', in, rather
than of, Africa, nevertheless illustrates the course
which European intrusion has usually followed in
orientalized Africa.   It was much more of an organized and civilized or semi-civilized State than the pirate

principalities of Northern Africa, but Lord Cromer at the beginning of his book lays stress upon its Oriental character, and, in one passage, lays down that 'the maximum amount of harm is probably done when an Oriental ruler is for the first time brought into contact with the European system of credit'.[1] This happened in the days of the Khedive Ismail, grandson of Mehemet Ali, who for thirteen years added £7,000,000 a year to the debt of Egypt, the actual annual revenue of Egypt being hardly more. All of this money was squandered except £16,000,000 invested in the Suez Canal. He held in his own hands or those of his family about one-fifth of the arable land of Egypt, which was largely cultivated by forced labour, and the condition of the Egyptian peasantry was desperate to the last degree. At length the crash came in 1876, when he could not meet his bills, and in 1879 he was forced to resign.

While Lord Cromer refers to Egypt as being an Eastern country, he also emphasizes the extent to which it had been penetrated by Europe. He speaks of it as an instance of a country 'where European civilization has, in a greater or less degree, been grafted on a backward Eastern government and society';[2] and in another place he says that 'Egypt may now almost be said to form part of Europe. It is on the high road to the Far East.'[3] Its position on the road from Europe to the East, and the cutting of the Suez Canal, greatly strengthened its connexion with Europe. He tells us that so far as it had been Europeanized, it had been Gallicized, European civilization penetrating in its French guise; that its population is heterogeneous and cosmopolitan to a degree almost unknown elsewhere, and that in no

[1] 1908 ed., vol. i, p. 58.  [2] Introduction, p. 5.
[3] Vol. i, p. 326.

country is there a greater variety of creeds. On the
other hand, according to Sir Valentine Chirol, the native
Egyptians are 'on the whole remarkably homogeneous',[1]
much more so than the natives of India. The Christian
Copts scarcely number one in thirteen millions. In
connexion with the demand for Egyptian independence, it should be borne in mind that 'We have to
go back to the doubtful and obscure precedents of
Pharaonic times to find an epoch when possibly Egypt
was ruled by Egyptians'.[2]

Ismail's extravagance led to bankruptcy and the bankruptcy led to international financial control, control by
the European creditors. One great feature of this
control was the establishment in 1876 of an International
European Commission of the Public Debt, the *Caisse de
la Dette publique*, which still exists; certain revenues
were earmarked to it, and it was given extensive powers
under the Law of Liquidation passed in 1880. The
Khedive had to give up all his lands; some of them, the
Daira lands, were already in the hands of his creditors,
and others, the Domains, he was forced to hand over;
while a fixed annual income was settled on him. He
was also compelled to accept the principle of responsible
ministers, which turned him, in name at any rate, from
a personal despot into a constitutional ruler. After his
resignation in 1879, his son Tewfik succeeded him. Then
came Arabi Pasha's rising, a military mutiny backed by
Nationalist sentiment. The French and English had
the largest interests in Egypt; the French refused to join
in armed intervention, the English went in alone, and
the result was British military occupation and British
predominance in Egypt.

[1] *The Egyptian Problem*, p. 156.
[2] *Modern Egypt*, ut sup., vol. i, p. 328.

The difficulty of the task was summed up by Lord Cromer in the words, 'One alien race, the English, have had to control and guide a second alien race, the Turks, in the government of a third race, the Egyptians'.[1] The relations of Egypt to Turkey constituted one great difficulty; the collapse of Egyptian authority outside Egypt proper, on the Red Sea littoral and in the Sudan, which had been hopelessly misgoverned, made another; and the presence of other Europeans in Egypt, in a preferential position, made a third and the greatest. The international safeguards existing prior to the British occupation became after that occupation so many obstacles to good government. Other European Powers were in a position to obstruct, and (before the great Franco-British understanding of 1904) very especially the French, who bitterly, and not unnaturally, in view of past history and of the lead which they had taken in the Suez Canal scheme, resented British control in Egypt and the continuance of British occupation. One great stronghold of Europeans in Egypt was the 'Capitulations', special extra-territorial privileges and immunities which foreign European residents had from old times enjoyed in the Turkish Empire.[2] Originally concessions or privileges given by a powerful Sultan to Europeans wanting to reside and trade in his dominions, in order to exempt them from the operation of the Sacred Law, in course of time they became formidable rights, a kind of *imperium in imperio*. The rulers of Egypt had extended these concessions further than was done elsewhere in the Ottoman Empire, and they had

[1] *ut sup.*, Introduction, p. 5.
[2] A full account of their origin and to what they grew in Egypt is given in all the books which have been mentioned. Reference should also be made to Appendix III.

become a grave abuse, graver in Egypt perhaps than anywhere else. They included immunity from ordinary taxation, other than custom duties, inviolability of domicile, exemption from the jurisdiction of the local courts. By the creation of mixed tribunals, which was prior to British occupation, and in various other directions after British occupation, these privileges or abuses were curtailed, but to a great extent they still exist in Egypt, the British Government, when it declared a Protectorate in 1914, holding out hope that they would be taken in hand after the War. As is shown in Appendix III, extra-territorial privileges of this kind were not and are not peculiar to the Turkish Empire. They exist, for instance, in China, and they existed in one form or another in European countries in the Middle Ages, before modern nations were fully formed, but the maximum of abuse seems to have been reached in Egypt. The Capitulations do not apply to the Sudan, owing to the elimination of Turkey from the Condominium.

After the British occupation of Egypt there were the beginnings of representative Institutions, a Legislative Council, and a General Assembly, which were merged in a Legislative Assembly in 1913, and Provincial Councils; but it was by practical rather than constitutional reforms, abolition of the lash and of forced labour, lightening of taxation on the peasantry, irrigation and so forth, that the British occupation benefited Egypt. The work of Lord Cromer will always stand out among the most beneficent and the most difficult chapters of administration in our overseas history. But in spite of beneficent results intrusion into Egypt, as elsewhere in North Africa, began as exploitation. Financial indebtedness of Egypt to Europe brought in European financial control, which was followed by European political control. All that can be said in condemnation of European methods and policy in this aspect will be found in a recent book, general in its treatment, by Mr. Leonard Woolf entitled *Empire and Commerce in Africa*.[1] The present pages have no concern with controversy, but it must be borne in mind that the exploited communities themselves arose out of, or were influenced by, previous alien intrusion. Furthermore, if Tunis, as it stands to-day under French Protectorate, or Egypt, as it has come to be since British occupation, could be placed before our eyes side by side with Tunis prior to French and Egypt prior to British intrusion, the general amelioration of native conditions might be held to justify European intervention.[2]

[1] Published by the Labour Research Department, 1919.

[2] Readers will bear in mind that the text dates from the early months of 1921 and therefore does not notice the most recent developments in Egypt.

# VIII

## SOUTH AFRICA

SOUTH AFRICA is commonly taken to be Africa south of the Zambesi, though in this chapter mention will be made of Northern Rhodesia, which is north of that river. If the mandated territory be included, all South Africa is now within the British Empire, except on the eastern side, where Portuguese East Africa comes down to a little below Delagoa Bay. The main geographical distinctions are between the low-lying coast regions and the high inland plateau, and between the desert west and the well-watered and mountainous east. The Tropic line runs through the north of the Transvaal, and touches the sea on the west just below Walfish Bay. Lord Milner tells us that the high plateau is, in spite of longer distance, more accessible from the south than from the east and west, ' For from the west, though the slopes are favourable, the intense aridity of the country makes progress difficult or impossible, and on the east there is a tremendous mountain barrier to be climbed'.[1] Hence European expansion has been in the main from south to north.

When we turn from the north to the south of Africa, we turn away from a borderland between Europe and Africa, and from an effete Orientalized Africa to that part of the continent which is most remote from Europe, and which was, when Europeans first appeared on the

---

[1] *The Nation and the Empire*, p. 224. Address on 'Geography and Statecraft', *ut sup.*

scene, a sphere of virgin barbarism.  European intrusion into South Africa did not come in the form of
exploitation, but in that of settlement and conquest, the
difference between South Africa, as a field for European
settlement, and North America or Australasia turning
on the numbers and the strong physique of the South
African natives.  It will be noticed that in South Africa
European settlement, starting at the point farthest
removed from Europe, has worked up towards Europe.
There does not seem to be any exact parallel on so large
a scale, though the first permanent European settlement
in Australia, on Sydney harbour, was on the side turned
away from Europe, and the first settlement in Vancouver
Island came not by expansion from the side next to
Europe but directly from the Pacific.  The reason, over
and above climate, for this trend of European settlement
in South Africa was that, though South Africa was not
an Orientalized Africa, and though it was not at first in
any sense a field for exploitation, yet the call of the East
influenced and, indeed, originated European intrusion
into South Africa.  For it was trade, and not African
trade, but trade with the East, which led to settlement
at the Cape.  Then, as Lord Milner has pointed out,
expansion into the interior was found to be easiest by
going due north.

The significance of South Africa for Europe was, for *The*
a very long time, simply that of being the turning-point on *Cape first settled by*
the high road from Europe to the East, and all the Euro- *the Dutch*
pean peoples who used the high road came of necessity *in connexion*
to the turning-point.  But for a century and a half they *with the East.*
came and went.  The Portuguese never established any
foothold at the Cape, and the first permanent station was
a Dutch station, formed by the Netherlands East India
Company in 1652, 165 years after the Cape had first

been sighted by Diaz ; and it was formed to forward the
trade with the East.   But, in order to make the station
as far as possible self-supporting, and to reduce the cost
of the garrison, a certain amount of settlement was
encouraged by the Directors of the Company ; Boers,[1]
i.e. farmers, made homes there, and in about thirty
years' time a very valuable addition to the small country
population was made in the form of French Huguenots,
vine-growers among them, who were sent out after the
Revocation of the Edict of Nantes in 1685.   A good
account of the Huguenot immigration is given by
Mr. Graham Botha, the Archivist of the Union of
South Africa, in his recent book, *The French Refugees
at the Cape*.   They were few in number ; the main wave
of immigration appears only to have brought in about
150, but many of the best-known names in South
Africa testify to Huguenot origin, Joubert, Cronje
(Cronier), de Villiers, du Plessis, Malan, Viljoen (Villion),
and others.   From this French immigration, Fransche
Hoek, the French corner, derived its name.   Under the
régime of the Netherlands East India Company, the
Cape was largely an outpost of the East and subordinate
to Batavia, present evidence of which is to be found in
some 20,000 Malays living in the neighbourhood of
Capetown.   The trading station and the country settlements more or less conflicted with each other, and at
the date of the first British occupation, in 1795, the
farmers of Graaf Reinet, then the farthest inland district, were in open revolt against the Government at
Capetown.   South Africa with its vast open spaces was
peculiarly favourable to trekking, and this (so marked
a feature in its history, among both Europeans and

---

[1] ' Boer ' is the same word as the German ' Bauer '.

natives) had begun before the English took over the Cape.

The Dutch were beforehand with the English in South Africa by 150 years, and when the English came in, they came in, so far as the Cape—not Natal—was concerned, forcibly over the heads of earlier European immigrants. But it was a curious kind of conquest. The first British armed occupation of the Cape, in 1795, followed upon the French conquest of the Netherlands, and the occupation was carried out in the name of the Prince of Orange, hereditary Stadtholder of the Netherlands, who at the time had taken refuge from the French in England. The Cape was given back to the Netherlands, though not to the Netherlands East India Company, by the Peace of Amiens in 1802; it was taken again in 1806, and finally ceded to Great Britain in 1814. But in the end it was really bought from the Dutch, as a part of a complicated general arrangement, by which Belgium was added to the Netherlands, and Great Britain paid to the Netherlands a sum of £6,000,000, as the price of keeping the Cape and British Guiana.[1]

*The British occupation of the Cape.*

By taking the Cape the English secured a field for settlement in Africa, but a field in which they had to deal both with a rival European race and with a native population. The Dutch had been so long in South Africa that they had been moulded by South Africa, and as South Africa is utterly unlike the Netherlands in all respects, it bred a type of Dutchmen very distinct from those of the mother country. At the time when Canada was taken by Great Britain, before the days of the French Revolution, the French Canadians were

*British and Dutch in South Africa.*

[1] See the note to p. 105, chap. iii of vol. iv, Part I, of the *Historical Geography of the British Colonies.*

directly under the French Crown. They had never re-
acted against the old régime, but the Dutch possessed a
tradition of freedom and independence. Except for the
few years between the two British occupations, they
were never directly under the Government of the
Netherlands, but under a great national company, the
Netherlands East India Company, and in opposition to
its restrictions had further developed the independent spirit. Moreover, their attitude towards the native
races was different from that which was becoming pronounced in Great Britain at the end of the eighteenth,
and beginning of the nineteenth century. The English,
in short, had to deal with a white race firmly rooted in
the land, at once very independent and very conservative, a difficult blend.

*The Albany Settlement.*    A large body of British immigrants, 4,000 or more,
was brought into the Cape exactly one hundred years
ago, in 1820-1. This immigration was known as the
Albany settlement, and the scene of the settlement was
the east of the Cape Colony, the settlers being landed
at Algoa Bay, where Port Elizabeth grew up as the outlet for the newly-settled districts. This gave to the
eastern part of the colony a strong British leaven, while
the west remained overwhelmingly Dutch ; and in this
respect the Cape Colony became to some extent
analogous to Canada with its French province of
Quebec and British province of Ontario. But, though
division into two separate colonies was talked of, it was
never carried out. The new settlers were planted on
the side nearest to Kaffirland, but Dutch farmers were
also on this border.

*Boers, British, and Natives.*    A remarkable book, entitled *The Bantu, Past and
Present*, has lately been published, written by a Bantu,
Mr. Molema. In it he says that the South African race

conflict has been dual, a struggle between Boer and
Briton, and a struggle between black and white, and
that the former, the struggle between the two white
races, was always 'comparatively negligible'.[1] This is
a strong statement to make, in view of the dimensions
which the rivalry between Boer and Briton attained, but
it cannot be doubted that the problem of the relations
between whites and natives is incomparably the more
vital and far-reaching of the two problems; moreover,
the struggle between Boer and Briton has largely arisen
out of the different attitude of the two peoples towards
the native races. As has been stated in the second
chapter, the natives with whom Europeans came into
contact at the Cape in the earlier years of European
settlement were the Bushmen and the Hottentots. The
Bushmen were natives of very primitive type, living by
hunting, and apparently the prey of all the other races,
coloured, or white. In course of time, they were largely
exterminated. The Hottentots were in a higher grade,
a pastoral people, with sufficient sense of ownership to
resent being ousted by the Dutch from their grazing
lands in the Cape Peninsula; their attitude led to the
Dutch going through the form of buying the lands. But
they were vagrant and disorganized, nor were they, to the
same extent as the Kaffirs, a fighting people; so they
became in a measure serfs to the Dutch, without being
actually enslaved. If we allow for the much later date
at which British settlement in Australia began, the relations of the early settlers in South Africa and in Australia
towards the natives whom they came across were on
much the same lines. There was plenty of room for
both whites and natives, plenty of opportunities too for

[1] *The Bantu, Past and Present*, S. Molema (W. Green & Son,
1920), p. 259.

cattle raids, and reprisals; there was little regard by the white men for the lives or rights of the natives.

For a long time the Dutch did not come into touch or conflict with the Kaffirs, the Bantu race. The Kaffirs were coming down and the Europeans were working up. They were both latter-day immigrants into South Africa. The van of the Bantus on the eastern side, the main side of the Bantu advance, was led by the Kosa or Ama Xosa Bantus, and in 1778 the Dutch Governor of the day made an agreement with some of their chiefs fixing the Great Fish river, some distance north-east of Algoa Bay, as the boundary between the colony and Kaffirland. It was still the boundary when the English took the Cape in 1806, and remained the boundary till 1819. Thus for forty years the white men did not move forward the boundary on this side, and the Kaffir wars, of which the fifth was in 1818-19, were much more the result of the Bantus pressing over the line than of European intrusion. About this time the Zulu chief, Chaka, had consolidated his military power and was pressing or threatening the Kosa Kaffirs behind. They had, therefore, a sufficient motive for moving on. After this war of 1818-19, the colonial boundary was carried forward, but not for a great distance, taking in only such territory as the Kaffirs had taken from the Hottentots; and, moreover, the strip of Kaffir land, which was annexed to the colony, was intended to serve as neutral territory. Then came, at the end of 1834, a great irruption of Kaffirs into the colony, with the results to which reference has been made in a previous chapter. The Kaffirs were in due course driven out; there was a counter invasion, and a large wedge of Kaffir territory, as far as the Kei river, was annexed under the name of the province of Queen

Adelaide. Orders were then sent from England to give it back, the blame being laid on the colonists, not the Kaffirs. It was given back, with the result that in later years all had to be done over again. For various reasons the Dutch were already ill content with British administration ; the retrocession and the charges made against the colonists, though they were made against British as well as Dutch and involved the British Governor, Sir Benjamin D'Urban, after whom the port of Durban was named, filled the cup of Boer bitterness, and the Great Trek took place which altered the whole history of South Africa. Writing from the point of view of the natives and their missionary friends, Mr. Molema says that 'this reversal of Sir Benjamin D'Urban's policy by Lord Glenelg might have been inexpedient for the whites, under the circumstances, but it was not unjust, although the colonists regarded it as such, and regard it as one of the causes of the Boer Great Trek which soon followed, the Dutch section being especially infuriated'.[1] This is a temperate statement from one point of view, and the writer does not attempt to justify the warring Bantus ; but it might well have been qualified by admitting that retrocession was inexpedient in the interests of the natives as well as of the whites, subsequent history having abundantly proved that their salvation has lain in British tutelage and control. The other side, the side of the colonists, has once more been fully set forth in the latest volume of Professor Cory's history.[2]

There is neither time nor space here to follow up subsequent South African history. It can be summed up *South Africa since the Great Trek.*

---

[1] p. 103.

[2] *The Rise of South Africa*, 3rd vol. (Longmans, Green & Co., 1919).

as a history of successive Boer treks inland into native
territories, of British half-hearted pursuits, of the formation of separate Boer communities, of constant vacillation
by the British Government in its relations with those
communities, until at length it all culminated in the great
South African War. We have Natal settled from the
sea by British settlers—as shown by the British name
Durban, challenged by the Boers who came overland—
as shown by the Boer origin of the name Pietermaritzburg [1]; we have at a much later date the entry of Germany
into South-West Africa; we have the discoveries of
diamonds and gold, which meant the influx of large
numbers of white immigrants of all races (the Uitlanders),
to whom President Kruger was so diametrically opposed;
and, finally, there is the construction and extension of
railways, in Lord Milner's words, 'of incomparable
potency in South Africa, owing to the vast distances
which separate its chief centres of European settlement
and to its almost total lack of navigable waterways.' [2]

What the railways have pre-eminently done for South
Africa is to link on the peninsula to the main body of
the continent. At the present day British South Africa
is an immense sphere extending into the centre of Africa.
It includes a great self-governing dominion, the Union of
South Africa, a union, not merely a federation, of two
British colonies and two late Boer republics, now the
four provinces of Cape, Natal, Transvaal, and Orange
Free State. To this self-governing dominion has been
added, under the mandate system, what was German
South-West Africa. Side by side with the Union is
the Crown Colony of Basutoland, a purely native terri-

[1] Pietermaritzburg was christened after two Boer leaders, Pieter
Retief and Gerrit Maritz.
[2] *The Nation and the Empire*, ut sup., p. 226.

tory, the British Bechuanaland Protectorate and the Swaziland Protectorate, both native territories, and the two Rhodesias, also a protectorate, and still administered, under close supervision, by the British South Africa Company. Southern Rhodesia has a substantial white population with popular representation, but not (so far) responsible government. Northern Rhodesia, which is north of the Zambesi, is not a white man's country in the sense of being, like Southern Rhodesia, a field of settlement. It is rather—like tropical Africa in general for Europeans—a field of exploitation. Basutoland and the Protectorates are under the High Commissioner for South Africa, who is also Governor General of the Union.

Our present concern is the European partition and colonization of Africa. South Africa is the principal field in Africa of European colonization, and we have seen that it is marked by being a field where Europeans always have been and always must be side by side with natives, and where two strong European races are side by side—or three, if the Germans are taken into account. It may be well to sum up what has been said already by trying to answer three questions: (*a*) First, what has been the substantial difference between Briton and Boer? (*b*) Secondly, how far has the presence of the natives influenced the relations between Briton and Boer and shaped the history of South Africa? and (*c*) thirdly, what is to be said for or against European intrusion into South Africa?

It will be obvious that the Dutch in the Cape Colony cannot have relished cession to another power. The *What has been* conquest was the mildest form of conquest; the Nether- *the sub-* lands Government received a *quid pro quo* in money; *stantial difference* the Netherlands East India Company had done little *between*

*Briton
and Boer
in South
African
history ?*
enough for the Dutchmen at the Cape, and when the
English took over the Cape the Dutch civil population
did not number 30,000 in all.  Still it is human to resent
alien rule.  But, after making allowance for this, it seems
fair to say that the essence of the divergence between
the two white races in South Africa is to be found in
the conflict between the centrifugal tendencies of the one
race and the centripetal tendencies of the other.  The
Dutch have always been inclined to separate, the British
to unite and hold together.  We have said that the British,
in having to deal with the Dutch in South Africa, had to
deal with a people at once very conservative and very
independent.  Their independent spirit has undoubtedly
been fostered by their surroundings.  The Boer race
are a notable illustration of the extent to which the land
moulds the people.  In going to South Africa the Dutch
went to a land which was in all respects the extreme
antipodes of their old home—very spacious instead
of cramped, having little to do with the sea and
everything to do with an unlimited interior, a pastoral
region which suggested and lent itself to dispersion and
isolation; in short, a land quite alien in spirit and in
character to the closely-packed Netherlands, the product
of the sea and almost as much water as land.  The Dutch
settlers inherited an independent spirit and came from
a republican strain, and in South Africa the Dutch spirit
declared itself in a tendency to split up and split off,
and in a restiveness against a central government.
This is well brought out in the description of the Boers
put into the mouth of General Delarey in an article in
the *Round Table* of June 1916, entitled ' The Rebellion:
its background and results'.  The Union of South
Africa, with self-governing powers tantamount to practical independence, which was intended finally to put

an end to splitting off, has still left the extreme Boer Nationalists striving, if they cannot split up South Africa, to split off South Africa from the British Empire. The Boer instinct has been towards separation, the British instinct towards union, and the great political importance of the British occupation of Rhodesia was that it closed the door to further trekking to the north.

Together with the spirit of independence, and fostered by isolation, was and is the Boer Conservatism, as shown very especially in their treatment of native races. The Dutch are by no means more cruel or inhuman than other peoples; on the contrary, while slavery was in existence at the Cape, the slaves were, as a rule, treated with exceptional mildness. But the conviction which *How far has the native question affected the relations between Boer and Briton?* came to our own people as to the wickedness of slavery or anything akin to it, and the missionary enthusiasm for native rights, did not infect the Dutch. They had good reason to resent the meddling of missionaries, and they were confirmed in their own stubborn views when they trekked into the interior; the Grondwet of the South African Republic laid down baldly that there should be no equality between white and coloured in either Church or State ; coloured men are still prohibited from sitting in the Union Parliament; and an utterance, quoted in the newspaper, of a Boer Nationalist in the last Union Parliament shows that the attitude is still what it has always been among a very large section of the Boers, while it is said to be the attitude also of the Dutch Reformed Church. A reference to Mr. Molema's book will illustrate how strongly a thinking native differentiates between the Boer and British point of view on native questions. This is only a rough generalization, for there must of course be many South African Dutchmen who care for native interests more than many South African Britons, but, as a rough generalization, it seems to represent the facts. It was largely or mainly on a native issue that the splitting-off process began. It was largely or mainly Boer dealings with natives which led to the first annexation of the Transvaal; and all through the history of South Africa for a century past, native questions have been inextricably mixed with the political troubles between the two white races. Within the British Empire, in South Africa only, is to be found a self-governing dominion flanked by native territories still under the control of the home Government and wishing to remain under the home Government just as strongly as the extreme Dutch Nationalists desire to get rid of any connexion whatever with the home Government. In other words, the natives represent the political antipodes of the extreme Dutch Nationalists, and are, in a sense, more pro-British than the British South Africans themselves. It is not possible to avoid the conclusion that the native question has fundamentally affected the relations between the two white races.

*How far was the European intrusion into South Africa justified?* If the British had never gone to South Africa, there could have been no difficulties between British and Dutch in South Africa, and if the Dutch had never gone to South Africa there could have been no difficulties between whites and natives. What right had Europeans to intrude at all? And, if there was to be European intrusion, what right had the British to interfere with the first white comers? This is the old tiresome question, which is, however, specially easy to answer in the case of South Africa. There was and is room in South Africa for whites as well as blacks, and the main body of blacks, as has been pointed out, were comparatively recent immigrants, who had little more title to South Africa than the whites. If the Europeans had not come in and broken such powers as the Zulus and Matabele, presumably these Bantus would have carried on at will their appalling slaughter of other natives, and South Africa would have remained a field of barbarism. Or are we to argue that the natives would have been amenable to missionaries, that missionaries alone would have had a right to go in, and that if they were killed subsequently it would of course be regrettable but no more than a domestic difference between them and their misguided hosts, and certainly not a matter calling for intervention? It is impossible to argue the case. It cannot be doubted that Europeans had a perfect right to go into and settle in South Africa, that the natives had no more right to molest them than they had to molest the natives, and that preserves for barbarism cannot be for ever maintained on the ground that when whites come among natives they always get the better of the natives. But it is possible to note the extent to which the whites have applied the maxim 'Might is right' (and not in Africa alone), and have assumed that, when they have gained control of a territory it is their territory, and its native inhabitants are there on sufferance and good behaviour. After the first annexation of the Transvaal the Boer leaders petitioned the British Government in almost pathetic terms that *their* country should be given back to them. Yet they were only a handful of whites among the natives, and immigrants of less than fifty years' standing. No one suggested a royalty to the natives for the diamonds of Kimberley or the gold of the Transvaal—and with some reason, for unless the white men had come and opened up the diggings and mines the diamonds and gold would have served no purpose, or rather, no commercial purpose. There is no other conclusion to the matter than that the white men must exercise tutelage and control over the coloured men until the coloured men rise to the standard of the white men, but they are bound to recognize their trusteeship and its responsibilities, and in such a case as that of Basutoland it has been admirably and adequately recognized.

But if we can make an excellent case for Europeans coming into South Africa on the common-sense ground that, as there was plenty of room for them, they had a perfect right to make their home there, what excuse was there for the British coming in, treading on the heels of the Dutch and taking over the government of the Cape Colony from them? It must always be remembered that the English did not oust the Dutch on the coast-line of Natal; Durban was of purely British origin. But as to Cape Colony, in the first place there was abundant room for any number of British immigrants, and they had as much right to come in side by side with Dutch and natives as the Dutch had to come in by the side of the natives. Still, it may be argued that they had no right to take the government from the Dutch. Whose land was it then? Did it belong to the natives or the Dutch? And if the natives had any rights can it be reasonably doubted that the native interests were better served by British than by Dutch administration? The Dutch attitude to South African natives—the attitude of absolute and unquestioned inequality, not involving by any means as a consequence inhuman treatment—has, it is true, been defended in Dr. Theal's last book, recently published; but the native writer already quoted does not share this view. If, on the other hand, we assume, as treaties assume (with the modification recently introduced by the mandate system), that these native lands are – speaking generally—at the disposal of the white governments which have annexed them, then the excuse for the British taking the Cape from the Dutch is simply that they took it as one of those bargains which come in the settlement of all wars, and that it was at least as justifiable here as at other times and elsewhere. The present writer does not feel qualified to sit in judgement on past history. No doubt in the Napoleonic Wars the Netherlands suffered'for the crime of being weak, and the strong had then, as now, the main voice in the settlement after the wars ended. But weak governments have in history been the most injurious to the interests of the governed, and only in so far as the British Government was weak and vacillating in South Africa—vacillating to a pitiable degree—did it fail to justify the supplanting of the very weak régime of the Dutch.

# IX

## WEST AND EAST AFRICA

### (1) *West Africa*

KEEPING to our rough division, borrowed from M. Jules Cambon, of European oversea possessions into colonies of settlement and colonies of exploitation, which very roughly corresponds to the difference between colonies in the true sense and dependencies, we have seen that North Africa is a sphere both of settlement, as in Algeria, and of exploitation, but more of exploitation than of settlement, while South Africa is primarily a sphere of settlement, not of exploitation. When we come to West and East Africa, with rare exceptions, such as the highlands of the Kenya Colony, we are dealing with spheres of exploitation solely; in tropical lands, where tropical conditions are intensified, Europeans go to administer, trade, and develop the resources, but not to live.

West Africa was the coast where the modern exploitation of Africa began, and the slave-trade was exploitation in its vilest form, directed to making money out of flesh and blood, not out of the products of the soil. It brought a medley of Europeans to the coast, the natives had every opportunity of comparing them and finding out who was worst or least bad, and it had the effect of setting the black man against the white, in addition to confirming him in his own practice of perpetual tribe warfare.

The abolition of the trade left the coast in a derelict condition. Europeans had done nothing to counteract barbarism; on the contrary, they had supported it. There were tribal states or communities which were horrible parodies of humanity, such as Ashanti, Dahomey, and Benin, and the British Government was in two minds whether or not to leave the coast altogether. Two-thirds of the nineteenth century in West Africa was spent in undoing or trying to undo the mischief which had been done; but then a time of real forward movement began. On this side of the continent, except in the Congo State, the scramble for Africa was by no means a bad thing. It forced the leading European Powers to define what had been indefinite. It confined them respectively within limits which were very gradually placed beyond dispute, and it made them responsible within those limits. In other words, it substituted some kind of order for chaos or for unadulterated barbarism. This applies to the coast region, not necessarily to the interior, where, as in Northern Nigeria, might be found organized Mohammedan sultanates. Similarly the growing demand in Europe for African products, while it led to the gravest abuses in the Congo, worked on the West Coast much more good than harm. It is all very well to rail at capitalism, but trade of every kind comes under this heading; all trade is liable to lead to evils in one form or another, yet without trade progress is impossible. Through the demand for West African palm-oil and kernels money flowed into as well as out of West Africa, and directly or indirectly the natives benefited. Roads and railways provide access to markets for natives as well as Europeans. Natives as well as white men benefit directly through the advance in tropical medicine and sanitation, and moreover it means that a good stamp of white men are encouraged to go out to West Africa.

The Government has lately been much criticized for placing an export duty on palm kernels, which is refunded if they are sent to England. The great market for these kernels before the War was Hamburg, and, in order to establish the trade at home and induce British capitalists to lay out money on the necessary plant and machinery, a pledge of preference was given for a certain term in the form of these export duties. It is contended that they are objectionable on free trade grounds, that they prohibit the natives from selling their produce in the most profitable market, and that native interests are being sacrificed to those of British capitalists. Whatever are the rights and wrongs of the matter, there cannot be much amiss with British administration when what would be a matter of course in the policy of other nations (preference to the protecting or controlling European Power) is denounced with us as a gross injustice to the native African.

*France and Great Britain in West Africa.* Before the War the three strong European Powers in Africa—France, Germany, and Great Britain—all met in West Africa, and only in West Africa. The two German West African dependencies, Togoland and the Cameroons, both had a British colony or Protectorate on one side, a French on the other. France and Great Britain are now wholly predominant in West Africa, and, while before the War France controlled a very much larger area of West African territory than did Great Britain, the disproportion is still greater now. Further, all the four British West African dependencies are entirely severed from each other, while the whole of the immense French West African Empire is joined together. There appear to be two main divisions of the French territory, each under a governor-general. *French West Africa*, the earliest nucleus of which was the Senegal, and *French Equatorial Africa*, the earliest nucleus of which was the Gaboon. The governor-general of the first has his headquarters at the fortified naval station of Dakar; the governor-general of the second at Brazzaville on the Congo. The first has seven or eight divisions or colonies under him, one of which, the Senegal, sends a deputy to the French Parliament; the second has four. Of the four British dependencies, three—the Gambia, Gold Coast, and Nigeria—are now enclaves in French territory; the fourth, Sierra Leone, has Liberia on one side. In the process of give and take between France and Great Britain, Great Britain has more than once made cessions to France in West Africa, as a set-off to some gain elsewhere. The best illustration is the famous 1904 Convention, noticed previously. The preamble states that the two Powers have resolved: 'to put an end, by a friendly arrangement, to the difficulties which have arisen in Newfoundland'; and the fourth article, coming after the articles referring to Newfoundland, states that the British Government recognizes that 'in addition to the indemnity referred to in the preceding Article, some territorial compensation is due to France in return for the surrender of her privilege' in Newfoundland. Then follows the territorial compensation, all in West Africa. Similarly, and presumably because of the gains which have accrued to Great Britain elsewhere as the result of the late War, the French have acquired by far the larger share of Togoland and the Cameroons, which were conquered jointly by the two Powers.

*The
British
West
African
Depen-
dencies.*
But, though not a little has been ceded in West
Africa, and though all the four British West African
dependencies are entirely isolated from each other and
almost entirely encircled by the French, they are very
good illustrations of the British capacity for what un-
friendly critics would call 'picking out the eyes'. In
the Gambia, the smallest by far of the four and the
northernmost, we hold the best navigable waterway in
West Africa for 240 or 250 miles from the sea; in
Sierra Leone, the best roadstead; on the Gold Coast,
great mineral and agricultural wealth; in Nigeria, the
lower basin and the outlet to the sea of the greatest
West African river; while Lagos, the main port of
Nigeria, is a marvellous centre of trade carried both
by water and by land. Our connexion with the Gambia
and the Gold Coast dates from the very beginning of
British overseas enterprise; with Sierra Leone, from
the beginning of the reaction against the slave-trade;
with Lagos from the time when Great Britain was
active in putting down the slave-trade; while Nigeria,
exclusive of Lagos, is quite a latter-day acquisition, and
dates from the scramble for Africa. Nigeria is the
one part of West Africa in which a modern British
chartered company, the Royal Niger Company, made
history. It is also interesting as illustrating the fact
that the tendency to make larger units, which has been
such an outstanding feature in the self-governing part
of the Empire, has also been at work on the dependency
side of the Empire, Nigeria, as it now stands, being
a combination of three separate units, the colony and
protectorate of Lagos, the protectorate of Southern
Nigeria, and the protectorate of Northern Nigeria, the
whole comprising an area of 335,000 square miles with
over sixteen millions of inhabitants.

What common features have these four possessions ? *Colony and Protectorate.*
They are all of them mixtures of colony and protec-
torate. That is to say, parts of them have been
formally annexed and made British soil, so that the
natives in these parts are legally British subjects, while
other areas are British protectorate, and in consequence
the natives are not in the eye of the law British subjects.[1] On the Gambia only a very few square miles
of the territory are colony, and the rest is protectorate,
and most of the colony has for administrative purposes
been tacked on to the protectorate. In Sierra Leone,
less than one-seventh of the territory is colony and the
rest protectorate, and here again some of the colony
has been absorbed in the protectorate. The Gold Coast
originally was all protectorate, except the actual soil
on which the old forts stood, and the protectorate only
grew up very gradually and quite voluntarily. Shortly
before 1830 the charge of British interests on the Gold
Coast was handed over by the Government to a committee of London merchants. They appointed as local
governor a very remarkable Scotsman, Captain George
Maclean. He had only a few police and no legal
authority outside the immediate neighbourhood of the
forts, but he set up a court of justice, and the natives
had so much confidence in him that they came from all
sides to accept his jurisdiction. This was followed by
formal treaties with various chiefs accepting British
jurisdiction, and in this way a protectorate began and
widened, its source being confidence in and a desire
for British justice, as administered by a singularly
capable and upright man. At the present day, however, there is more colony and less protectorate on the
Gold Coast than in the other three dependencies, for

[1] See Appendix II.

in 1901 the whole of what had been the old Gold Coast protectorate was annexed, and, as the result of the last of several Ashanti wars, Ashanti, which lies behind it, was annexed also. Behind Ashanti there is a further protectorate, the Northern Territories. In Nigeria there is a small bit of colony, the part of the old Lagos colony and protectorate which had been annexed, and there is an immense area of protectorate, or rather of two protectorates, southern and northern. In all the four dependencies the governor is governor of the whole territory, colony and protectorate alike; the colony in each case has a legislative council, and, speaking very roughly either the legislative council of the colony may pass laws for the protectorate, or the governor legislates for it and applies at his discretion the laws passed for the colony. In this respect Ashanti, though it is colony and not protectorate, is treated as if it were a protectorate. The distinguished Frenchman who has been already quoted says that ' In colonization the English have method but not system ',[1] and this saying may fairly be applied to British administration in West Africa. Like the Romans, we are happily ' not cursed with the passion for uniformity ' and protectorate has the advantage of admitting more elasticity in administration than colony.

There is a common defence force for all the West African dependencies, known as the West African Frontier Force, units of which are stationed in all four, varying in strength from a company in the Gambia to several battalions in Nigeria. In normal times this force is under the Colonial Office, not the War Office, and its chief officer is an inspector-general. It did notably good service in the War, both in West and in

[1] Cambon, *ut sup.*, p. 144.

East Africa, and some battalions had been intended for service in the East, when the armistice came. Sierra Leone differs from the other three West African dependencies in being an imperial naval station, and, over and above the Sierra Leone battalion of the West African Frontier Force which serves the protectorate, there is a garrison of regular troops at Freetown, including one or other of the two battalions of the West India regiment, which is always stationed there.

All these West African possessions are alike in being among the richest and most prosperous parts of the whole Empire. The great staple source of wealth in West Africa has been palm oil and kernels, used for soap, candles, and the like, together with (especially on the Gambia) the oil-producing ground-nuts; but on the Gold Coast an imported industry, cocoa, has now quite superseded palm oil, and a very large proportion of the world's supply of cocoa comes from the Gold Coast. It is a native-grown industry, and directly enriches the natives. Ashanti produces cocoa among other products, and those who attack European intrusion into Africa might do well to contrast Coomassie as it now is, a growing centre of trade, with its condition twenty years ago under Prempeh's militant barbarism.[1] There are various other sources of wealth—agricultural, timber, and minerals. On the Gold Coast, gold is the oldest and manganese a recent export, and in Nigeria tin and coal are found.

It is a long distance from the Gambia to the Cameroon mountain, now attached to Nigeria, and there are necessarily many varieties of native races under British

---

[1] We have now a standard book on Ashanti in *A Vanished Dynasty: Ashanti* (John Murray, 1921), by Sir Francis C. Fuller, K.B.E., C.M.G., the late able Chief Commissioner of Ashanti.

supervision or direct control.  In Nigeria alone there
is the greatest difference between the Pagan tribes of
the South and the Mohammedan states of the North,
which were and are organized communities under
native rulers, who are guided but not supplanted under
British protectorate.  But everywhere the experience
during the War was much the same, that the natives
did not take advantage of war conditions to make
trouble.  On the contrary, they actively co-operated in
the struggle, and nowhere more so than in Northern
Nigeria, where, if there had been trouble, it would
have been most serious and far-reaching.  It is idle to
contend, in the face of this record, that British administration has not commended itself to the West African
natives, as idle as to argue that the wealth which comes
out of and enriches West Africa is evidence only of
profiteering capitalism.

*The West Africans have had an oppor- tunity of making com- parisons.* If then British administration has on the whole been
markedly successful in West Africa, to what is the
success due?  In the first place, the West African
natives have had unusual opportunities of making
comparisons—an important point.  It not infrequently
happens in our case that, after conquest and annexation,
tribes or peoples settle down with singular rapidity,
but that after an interval of a good many years they
show signs of discontent and unrest.  The explanation
seems to be that, as a rule, our coming gives them
a much better government, more security for life and
property, and more equal justice than they had before,
and knowing and comparing both régimes, they are
well content with the new régime.  Then comes a
generation who have never known any but the new
régime, and therefore cannot make any comparison,
and who, under the new régime, have learnt to expect

more than could possibly be hoped for under the old conditions; hence arise fresh demands and criticism of the existing authority if these demands are not complied with. On the West Coast many of the natives had opportunities of comparing, for instance, British and German administration, and when the War came, there were obvious signs that they preferred British to German control. In the next place we have, on the whole, a wider experience, a richer store of traditions and precedents, and a larger number of men trained in the administration of native races, than any other people. The French are rich in the same way, but not quite to the same extent, for India has been a wonderful training school for British administrators, and on the west coast of Africa we have lately drawn governors largely from the Malay Peninsula, one of the most successful spheres of British rule and pro- tectorate. In the last quarter of a century there have been three governors of the Gold Coast who served apprenticeship in the Malay Peninsula, including the late Governor, Sir Hugh Clifford, now Governor of Nigeria; latterly two successive Governors of Sierra Leone had graduated in the Malay Peninsula; and the Governor of Southern Nigeria, before it was amalgamated with Northern Nigeria, had also belonged to the Malay Peninsula Service. The man, however, whose name perhaps stands first among those of ad- ministrators in tropical Africa, Sir Frederick Lugard, learnt his trade in Africa. Last, but not the least factor in our success, there is the British temperament, with its liking for method rather than system. It is both difficult and invidious to attempt to compare French and British as administrators. It is impossible to avoid a patriotic bias. In the earliest days in West

Africa the French were reputed the best liked by the natives of all Europeans, and in our own times they have in various parts of the world been brilliantly successful. In Morocco, for instance, Marshal Lyautey seems to have achieved wonderful results. As road and railway makers they are in the first rank among nations. But it would probably be fair to say that, for good or ill, they are a more military people than the British, and in trade they are less inclined to the policy of the open door. Of all European peoples the British are least minded to drill and be drilled, and most minded to go their own ways and let others go theirs. This means that we do not worry native races unnecessarily, and work, as far as possible, through native channels and in accordance with native customs and traditions. In Northern Nigeria, under the wise guidance of such men as Sir Frederick Lugard, this has been most notably so. In the words of his successor, Sir Hugh Clifford, the more advanced states are each 'governed by its natural rulers, through its own institutions, and in accordance with its own immemorial traditions, laws, and customs'.[1] Under British rule, or Protectorate, native races have probably more day to day practical freedom than under any other overlordship. Overseas administration reflects the trend of public opinion in the home country, and the extent to which the Government of that country is amenable to public opinion. In the United Kingdom there is nothing that stirs public opinion so much as any policy or measure which can be construed as infringing liberty, and in no country is public opinion more potent. Hence the responsible men on the spot in the tropics, apart from their own British predilections, have a perpetual pressure

[1] *Address to the Nigerian Council*, 1920, p. 23.

put upon them to safeguard the liberties of the coloured races. In a book entitled, *Alone in West Africa*,[1] the author, Mrs. Gaunt, an Australian lady, a courageous traveller and picturesque writer, who paid a flying visit to the West Coast of Africa some four years before the War, was somewhat critical of British methods and inclined to contrast them unfavourably with the orderliness of the Germans and their stronger hand, as she found it in Togoland. But, after Togoland had been taken from the Germans in the first month of the War, in the part of Togoland which was placed for the time being under British administration, the area under cultivation increased in two years' time by 33 per cent., a fairly conclusive proof that the natives found British control more to their taste than German. Similarly, writing of the plantations in the Cameroon mountain districts, formerly German and now attached to Nigeria, Sir Frederick Lugard says that, under German rule, the labour was 'recruited by forced levies, and the German district officers continually protested that the country was becoming depopulated and villagers were migrating over the Nigerian border'.[2] On the other hand, Sir Hugh Clifford, in his recent address to the Nigerian Council of 29th December 1920,[3] stated that 'every petty chief and headman whom I met during my recent visit to Victoria and Buea was a frank and confirmed *laudator temporis acti*, for whom "German times" were synonymous with the easy years that men knew before the outbreak of the Great War. . . . In his own day the German was not loved in the Cameroons; yet now he is openly regretted—not for himself, but because he is to-day identified in the popular mind with

[1] *Alone in West Africa*, by Mary Gaunt (T. Werner Laurie).
[2] Cd. 468, 1920, p. 73.  [3] p. 210.

the pre-war conditions that vanished with the War.'
Comparison, therefore, is not always flattering to
British administration, but at the same time, these
outspoken complaints were in a sense a testimony to it.
If native chiefs had expressed to a German Governor
preference for British rule, they would have been dealt
with in very summary fashion.

*Historic continuity in the British connexion with the West Coast of Africa.*    The abolition of the slave-trade obviously made a
great break in the history of West Africa; but, not-
withstanding, it is interesting to note what a strong
strain of continuity remains in the record of our connexion with the West Coast. We went there, in the
first instance, like others, for trade; a particular kind
of trade came into existence, the slave-trade, and,
because we were keen and capable traders, we gained
an unlovely pre-eminence as slave-traders. The slave-
trade was carried on with America, and the late War
brought a revival of direct trade between West Africa
and the United States. The coast was a great source
of riches to British merchants in slave-trading times;
it is a great source of riches now, and at the very same
points which were trading centres in the days of the
slave-trade. At the present day, as was the case in
slave-trading times, Liverpool is the great port for
West African trade, and the acquisition inland of
Northern Nigeria, which marked a departure from the
old method of holding selected places on the coast
as trading centres, was again due to a merchants'
company. West Africa is a striking illustration of
successful trade preceding and leading to successful
administration, and the Gold Coast, peculiarly associated
with the slave-trade, is noteworthy both as a place in
which a representative of merchants first acquainted
the natives with British justice, and also as a dependency

where in our own day the natives themselves directly grow and supply and are enriched by a product wanted for European markets. The historical continuity is further illustrated by the fact, on which emphasis has already been laid, that all these British West African dependencies are separated from each other and bounded on the land side by the sphere of another European Power. It is true that Nigeria has a great, and the Gold Coast a substantial, expanse inland. But still they all look outward separately to the sea, they do not link up behind, as is the case with the French possessions, into a continuous continental Empire. The present, in our case, may be said to be the past writ very large, and seaborne traffic is still its outstanding feature. It has been suggested that future competition between French and British in this part of the world may take the form of competition between land and sea routes. If so, we may have reasonable confidence that we shall hold our own.

## (2) *East Africa.*

West Africa gives no opening for European settle- *West and East Africa contrasted and compared.* ment, unless an exception can be made in favour of the Cameroon mountain region, which has lately come into our possession. In East Africa this is not so. The Shiré highlands in Nyasaland provide living places for Europeans, though they are not a field for British colonization ; whether the mountain districts in the new British mandate province of Tanganyika will be so remains to be seen ; but on the highlands of the Kenya Colony, the late British East Africa Protectorate, it has been abundantly proved that British settlers and their families live, multiply, and thrive, and the very difficult problem of adjusting the respective rights of the resident white settlers and of the natives has in consequence arisen.　In West Africa we are side by side at every point with a powerful European neighbour and competitor, France.　In East Africa, Germany having been eliminated, we hold the field exclusively between Italian Somaliland and Portuguese East Africa, and have added under mandate to our own already strong position on this side of Africa, the commanding position which Germany held.　Our colonies and Protectorates, with which alone it is proposed to deal, and omitting Somaliland, are the Nyasaland Protectorate, Kenya Colony, Uganda Protectorate, the Protectorate of the Islands of Zanzibar and Pemba, with some mainland coast-line, and the mandated territory of Tanganyika, other than the north-west part, which has been assigned to Belgium.　It is an immense area, taken in all, and here there is the continuity which on the western side of the continent the French have, and we lack.

*The British possessions in East Africa are all modern.*　While our possessions in West Africa carry us back to the very earliest days of British overseas enterprise, our possessions in East Africa are all of them modern, dating from the scramble for Africa.　Before the eighties of the last century such influence as we had (and we had great influence) arose mainly through the relations of India to East Africa, and through our self-imposed mission to put down the slave-trade.　While on the west coast participation in the slave-trade was for many generations the great attraction for the English, it was hostility to the slave-trade which drew us to East Africa.　Through Livingstone's influence, Nyasaland became and still remains a great sphere of missionary enterprise, and another notable mission field, in which

Bishop Hannington lost his life, is Uganda, where both the zeal and the rivalries of Christian missionaries have been well illustrated. There is no exact parallel on the west coast to the rôle which missions have played in extending the Empire ; but Sierra Leone, the offspring of philanthropy, is somewhat analogous, and the record of the Baptist mission at Victoria in what was before the War the German Cameroons no doubt supplied an additional argument, if argument was needed, for replacing that district under the British flag. In East Africa, as in West Africa, we owe our large inland territory mainly to a chartered company. What the Royal Niger Company was to Northern Nigeria, that the Imperial British East Africa Company was to the British East Africa Protectorate, now the Kenya Colony, and to Uganda. In either place a great trunk railway was constructed, the Uganda railway from Mombasa to Lake Victoria being completed some years before the whole line from Lagos to Kano was opened. By coming into possession of German East Africa, we have secured another trunk line, the line from Dâr-es-Salaam to Kigoma on Lake Tanganyika. As in West Africa, so in East Africa, there is a single military force for all the dependencies, including Somaliland. This is the King's African Rifles, the first units of which were raised in Nyasaland. Many more likenesses and many differences between West and East Africa might be noticed. In parts of the low-lying country of East Africa the climate does not seem to be better than in West Africa. There is in East Africa no river which has so far proved as helpful as the Niger, with all its defects. But East Africa has a coast with good harbours, and access inland from water to water, from the ocean to the great lakes, is fairly good. It is bounded on the side of the interior by water, not by desert, and the northern lakes give water communication to the Sudan and Egypt. There is also off the coast of East Africa an island which history has proved to be of commanding importance, Zanzibar—a typical jumping-off place.

*Zanzibar.*   Sir Charles Eliot, in his book on *The East Africa Protectorate*, published in 1905,[1] speaks of Zanzibar as 'perhaps the richest and most beautiful spot in tropical Africa', but says its harbour is bad. In the Colonial Office list, on the other hand, the harbour is said to be one of the finest in Africa, and the *Admiralty Pilot*, which is the best authority on harbours, speaks of 'the excellent anchorage fronting the town'. It faces the mainland, and has been a great emporium of trade. Zanzibar rose to greatness when a Sultan of Muscat, in Arabia, whose predecessors had succeeded the Portuguese as the predominant Power on the East African coast north of Cape Delgado, reasserted the power, which had fallen into abeyance. In 1832 he proceeded to and established himself at Zanzibar, and after his death Zanzibar and East Africa were separated from Arabia altogether. Not a little of the wealth of Zanzibar came in the past from the slave-trade, slaves being brought from the interior to Bagamoyo, over against the island, very much along the same route as is now followed by the railway. The trade was rife, in spite of a treaty with Great Britain of 1845, until Sir Bartle Frere was sent on a mission to the Sultan in 1872, which resulted in the following year in an effective treaty. We have seen that the British and German Protectorates on the coast were obtained from and at the expense of the Sultan of Zanzibar, but that his claims were held to be limited inland. When the

---

[1] Published by Edward Arnold; see pp. 21 and 31.

British and Germans mutually settled their respective spheres, the Germans bought out their coast-line from the Sultan ; but we still recognized his legal rights over the coast-line of British East Africa to ten miles inland, leasing it and paying him an annual rental, and his rights were safeguarded in the recent Order in Council of 11th June 1920, which annexed the East Africa Protectorate, and constituted it the Kenya Colony. It excepts : ' such territories as form part of the Dominions of His Highness the Sultan of Zanzibar.'

The reason for annexing the territory behind the *The Kenya Colony,* coast-line is given in the Preamble to the Order in Council, which recites : ' Whereas British subjects have *the Uganda Protector-* settled in large numbers in the said territory,' and goes on to explain that it is therefore annexed with a view to *ate, and the Tan-* further development and more convenient administra- *ganyika Territory.* tion. In other words, a large part of this immense territory, all the high plateau on which the capital, Nairobi, stands, between 5,000 and 6,000 feet above the sea—the highest point reached by the Uganda railway being over 8,000 feet above sea-level—is a part of the world where Europeans can make and already have made permanent homes.

Let us look at the main features of the three great East African provinces which have come under British control. The Kenya Colony with the coast-line, which is held on lease, has an estimated area of rather under 250,000 square miles, and a population estimated at less than 2¾ millions. The Uganda Protectorate has an area of 109,000 square miles, including 16,000 square miles of water, and an estimated population of over 3,300,000. The whole of what was German East Africa has an area of 384,000 square miles, and a population of between seven and eight millions.

Thus Uganda is much the most thickly populated, and Kenya has by far the smallest population. Uganda is a purely inland province, having its main outlet to the sea by the Uganda railway, which runs entirely not through Uganda, but through East Africa, to its ocean terminus at Mombasa; but the Protectorate has a back-door by the Upper Nile and the Sudan, which may be of far greater value and importance in future years than it is at present. Not only is this inland province the most thickly populated, but the natives, or some of them, are more civilized and on a higher level than the tribes and peoples farther east. Uganda proper, which gives its name to the whole Protectorate, though it is only one of various native states or communities in the Protectorate, is a native kingdom, and the young Kabaka or king, who paid a visit to England shortly before the War and came to his majority and his kingdom just as the War broke out, has his rights secured by treaty. He is a Christian, along with a large proportion of his subjects. As this Protectorate is at once more thickly peopled and has more political organization than East Africa, so in the Tanganyika province the most thickly populated districts are in the north-west of that province, on the borders of Uganda, the native Sultanates of Urundi and Ruanda, which have been assigned to Belgium, and in which are some $3\frac{1}{2}$ millions out of the seven to eight millions in the whole province. Thus it is in the interior that the native Africans hold the field most, and the climate suits them; and in Uganda Europeans come to administer and to form plantations, but not to be permanent residents. Uganda is rich in tropical products, cotton heading the list. In past years some parts of the Protectorate were ravaged by sleeping-sickness, and it has been a great field of white medical effort and research as well as of spiritual missionary work. The latest estimates give about 850 Europeans in the Uganda Protectorate. This would include all the missions and Government officials in addition to planters. Before the War the white population of German East Africa was estimated at about 5,000, and this total was said to include over 900 women and over 700 children. It has been said that the Germans took their wives and families out to the African tropics more than our people have been in the habit of doing, and the proportion of officials and soldiers was probably higher with them than with us. But these figures, which include other Europeans as well as Germans, look as if parts of Tanganyika, such as the Usumbara region, are favourable to European settlement, and a German professor, in a lecture given in London in January, 1914, was of the opinion that German East Africa would be 'a mixed colony like Natal and Rhodesia'.[1] Most of the province, however, especially the lowlands on the coast and in the far interior on the great lakes and in the basin of its main river, the Rufiji, with its affluents, which forms about a quarter of the territory, is malarious and unhealthy, and a prey to the tsetse fly. The plantation products include sisal, coffee, and rubber. In the East Africa Protectorate, as it then was, the census of 1911 gave 3,175 Europeans, of whom 995 were at Nairobi, the capital of the territory. The latest figures to hand give 5,570 Europeans, of whom 2,000 are at Nairobi. Therefore the Europeans, though still a handful, have grown steadily in numbers. The

[1] See paper on 'German Colonial Policy', by Professor Moritz Bonn, of Munich University, 13th January 1914, *United Empire*, 1914, pp. 126-42.

whites include some South African Boers, and there are
or were some Boers also in the Tanganyika territory.
The census of 1911 also credited the East Africa Protectorate with nearly 12,000 Asiatics, and they are now
returned as over 17,000. There are between 3,000 and
4,000 Asiatics in Uganda. Indian traders have for long
past been a very important element on the east coast of
Africa. There are two outstanding centres in the
Kenya Colony and adjoining coast protectorate, the
upland centre and seat of administration, Nairobi, and
the coast town of Mombasa with its two harbours, of
which Kilindini on the south-west of Mombasa island
is the harbour for ocean-going steamers and trade.

*Euro-*
*peans and*
*natives in*
*Kenya*
*Colony.*
The native races in the Kenya Colony are very various.
There are Somalis in the north-east, Arabs on the coast,
and the mixed breed known as Swaheli; there are
Bantu-speaking tribes and peoples, and there are what
Sir Charles Eliot calls Nilotic tribes or races, akin to
the peoples of the Nile basin. Among the last are the
Masai, of whom, though they are not very many in
number, we hear much in connexion with East African
questions, because they appear in the areas where
Europeans have come in. According to Sir Charles
Eliot's account, some of them, when he wrote his book,
had settled down and become agriculturists, but the
majority of them, whom he styles the Masai proper, he
describes as 'pastoral nomads who recognize only two
things as worthy of their care and interest, namely,
cattle and warfare'.[1] Pastoral peoples, of more or less
nomad habits, obviously require more land for their
grazing and their movement than do settled agriculturists, and tribes of this kind are more difficult to deal
with than organized native communities such as are

[1] p. 134.

found in Uganda. Further, tropical regions at a high altitude which are good for grazing attract Europeans and their stock as well as natives, and then comes the white man's demand for large concessions. Thus, with the influx of Europeans into areas where the Masai were in a kind of spasmodic possession, the difficulties as to the disposal of lands were great, and claims made by or on behalf of the natives had to be weighed against the demands of the incoming white men. The general solution in such cases is found in constituting native reserves, within which the land is secured in perpetuity to the natives and cannot be alienated to white men. The natives are not compelled to live in them, but outside them they have no specially vested rights, and inside them they keep their own tribal customs and tenures. The duty of the Government, as trustee for the natives, is to ensure that the land within the reserves is ample, and that the reserves are not relegated to the barren and waterless parts of the country, leaving the pick of the grazing areas to the white men. There is, in short, a conflict of considerations. If the most and the best is to be made out of a country and its resources, this end is more likely to be achieved by letting or selling the land to white farmers than by leaving it to uncivilized natives. On the other hand, the natives cannot, without gross injustice, be rendered landless and deprived of their means of living. In 1904 the Deputy Commissioner wrote: 'The Masai will never give us serious trouble, as long as we treat them fairly and do not deprive them of their best and favourite grazing grounds.'[1] At this date the question was being discussed of concessions to Europeans in this particular area, one of which was as large as 500 square miles.

[1] *Africa*, No. 8, 1904, Cd. 2099, p. 6.

But where a territory is adapted both to white men and to coloured, there is another burning question beside that of the land—the labour question. If a country is to be developed it must be worked, and grants of land to Europeans for agriculture or for cattle and sheep-farming are of little avail, if there is no sufficient supply of labour. Then arises a demand from the white men for the native labour which, if the natives are willing to work, can be supplied on the spot; there is, too, the temptation to make them work if they are not willing. This labour question has been to the front lately in East Africa. The traditional British policy has been, and, it is to be hoped, always will be, entirely opposed to compulsory labour for private employers, though there may be a case for legal compulsion in certain areas for Government purposes on roads and public works within carefully defined limits. Such work is in effect a form of tax paid in personal service. Forced labour is closely akin to slavery, and can be and has been a great engine of oppression and abuse, especially if the labourer is sent to work at a long distance from his home. It was practised ruthlessly in Egypt under the old régime, and in the Belgian Congo, and was one of the defects of German administration in Africa. It may be unavoidable when the employer is the Government, but even then it is open to objection, and in the case of private employers it is wholly inadmissible. On the other hand, those who know the natives best, and have their interests most at heart, hold that by accustoming them to work, by creating among them habits of steady industry, and awakening among them the wants which civilized men have (at the same time providing the means in the form of wages for supplying these wants)—by these means, and only by these means, will they be raised to a higher plane. Accordingly, a late dispatch from the Secretary of State,[1] dealing with the labour question in East Africa, laid down that the natives in the reserves should be advised to go to work, and this has been criticized on the ground that advice by the Government conveyed through the chiefs will be taken as an order, and that the result will be in effect forced labour. The remedy would seem to lie in constant and close supervision by an adequate staff of officials who thoroughly know the natives, and who will ensure that no one is taken to work against his will.

In most countries, whether white or coloured lands, good employers will nearly always in the long run get men to work for them. A recent account speaks of labour in East Africa as plentiful and fairly cheap, and anything like force conflicts with the real interests of employers as well as workmen. Ruling out forced labour, as it must be ruled out, if natives cannot be induced to take work for good wages and on equitable terms, there are the two alternatives of not developing the country or of importing labour. The cost of importing white labour would be prohibitive, and the white man would soon want to set up for himself, while the importation of coloured labour leads to opposition, which was shown in its most violent form when Chinese labour was imported to work the South African gold mines. In various tropical possessions of the Empire East Indians have been by far the most satisfactory form of imported labour, and they have long been connected with East Africa. But the particular case which we are considering is that of the Highlands, not the low-lying parts of East Africa, and Sir Charles

[1] See Cmd. 873, August 1920.

Eliot's book shows that he would not bring Indians in to the Highlands, so as not to have them competing with Europeans in what is a field for European colonization, and in a climate which is probably better suited to Europeans than to Indians. Moreover, Indians have come into East Africa as traders, not as plantation hands. This much has been said to show the difficulties which are presented by this particular area of tropical Africa. One school of thought, as represented in Mr. Woolf's book on *Empire and Commerce in Africa*, is quite content to regard the whole business as an instance of capitalist greed, whereby natives are deprived of their lands and reduced to serfdom. But there is another point of view. Are these lands to lie fallow and not to produce what they can be made to produce? Are the natives to be left as we originally found them? Or are they to be made useful and productive in their own interests as well as in the interests of the world at large? Anyhow, great importance must be attached to the presence of well-organized missions in East Africa, as also in Nyasaland. If white settlers and planters can bring strong influence to bear upon the Government on the spot and in England in support of their own views and interests, the case of the natives does find and is sure to find effective support from the missionary bodies which have no object to serve beyond the welfare of those among whom they are at work.

*Nyasa-land.* There is only space to say a few words of Nyasaland, in area about one-third larger than Scotland (nearly 40,000 square miles), with a native population of the most varied elements, numbering over 1,100,000, of whom barely 800 are Europeans. It is geographically the link between South and East Africa. It is almost a legacy from Livingstone and the scene of many missions, notably the two Scottish Missions and the Anglican Universities Mission to Central Africa. It has highlands and lowlands like East Africa, but the Shiré highlands have a much lower average level than the East African plateau. It is a land of tropical agriculture, including cotton, tobacco, and tea, cotton cultivation being carried on by natives as well as Europeans. White planters, so far, have not had great difficulty in securing labour, the interests of the native workmen being carefully safeguarded by Government regulations. The great difficulty of the protectorate has been noticed in Chapter VI—want of good communication with the outer world.

NOTE.– Since this chapter was written, there have been further developments in regard to both the Labour and the East Indian questions in Kenya Colony.

# X

## THE LATE CAMPAIGNS IN AFRICA

THE late War was carried directly or indirectly into all parts of Africa. The Germans owned African possessions on east, west, and south-west. The Turks had claims and influence in the north and had lost Tripoli only two or three years before the War. The Germans would have been glad to rule Africa out of the War, and some kind of overtures were made to that end, for the very good reason that in Africa they stood inevitably to lose. The argument was that the fate of Africa must in any case depend upon the fighting in Europe, and that therefore it was superfluous to carry the War into Africa. But for the Allies to have consented to a truce in Africa would have meant leaving intact to Germany sea bases and powerful wireless stations, such as the great high power station at Kamina in Togoland, which had only been opened two or three days before the War began, and which Sir Hugh Clifford described as 'destined to be the pivotal point of the German world-wide wireless system'. German intelligence and German facilities for raiding Allied commerce would have thereby gained immeasurably. Moreover, it was obvious that, with German Africa in their hands, the Allies would have valuable assets for barter at the end of the War, should that end fall short of complete victory.

As they could not keep Africa out of the War, by inciting against us the Turks and through them the Moslems, and by fostering irreconcilable Boer nationalist sentiment, the Germans added to the campaigns which they fought themselves, a Turkish invasion of the Suez Canal and Egypt, the Senussi rising in Libya, the Darfur rising in the Sudan, native risings against the French in the region of Agades and elsewhere in Central Africa, and the South African rebellion. Every effort was made to raise Africa against the Allies. In view of the strength of Moslem fanaticism when aroused by calls to a holy war, it is very remarkable that German and Turkish intrigues produced so little effect. The Mohammedans in the British colonies and protectorates took very little notice of the entry of Turkey into the War. In Northern Nigeria, for instance, the Mohammedan Emirs were solid for Great Britain and claimed, like the princes of India, to have a partnership in the War. One factor on our side, no doubt, was the experience which African pilgrims to Mecca remembered of Turkish exactions at the port of Jeddah and on the route to the Holy Places; on the contrary we did what we could to safeguard them, and the returning pilgrims bore witness in our favour. The Sultan of Darfur was almost a solitary exception in going into revolt, and, for one cause or another, he was disaffected before the War began.

Of the four campaigns against the four German *Features* possessions in Africa, South-West Africa was, on land, *of the* conquered by white troops alone and by South Africans *cam-* *paigns* alone. The King's ships kept the sea and transported *against* or safeguarded the transport of the troops that attacked *the* *African* from the seaboard, but otherwise General Botha and *depen-* his South African officers and men were solely respon- *dencies of* sible. No European allies co-operated and no coloured *Germany.* troops took part in the actual fighting. Togoland and the Cameroons were both conquered by converging

British and French forces, and in the Cameroons a small Belgian detachment was with the French. In both campaigns the rank and file of the fighting forces were coloured men, and almost entirely West Africans led by white officers. In the Cameroons we had one battalion of Indian soldiers, and a small white artillery unit was sent from England, together with some white engineers, signallers, and the rest; the water played a great part in this campaign, and on shore naval guns and gun parties were used, but in the main the campaign was carried through by West African soldiers. In East Africa we had as allies the Belgians on the west and north-west, and after a while the Portuguese on the south, but we had no strong partner to share the burden of the campaign, as we had in the French on the other side of Africa. Our sailors were busy both on the ocean and on the great lakes, and our land forces were very representative of the Empire. In the early days, white troops of the line were employed; the Indian army was well represented; South Africans represented the Dominions; Rhodesia sent both white and coloured fighters. The King's African Rifles and other East African troops were supplemented, when the Cameroons campaign was over, by a Nigerian brigade, the Gold Coast regiment and the Gambia company from the West African Frontier Force; and both the West India regiment and the British West Indies regiment were represented. The forces contained both white and coloured units, but as the campaign went on, for climatic reasons, and because the white troops were badly wanted elsewhere, it became more and more a coloured men's fight.

*Togoland.*    The first of the campaigns was in Togoland. It was a very small affair, over in about a fortnight, and it hardly deserves the name of a campaign. Here the Germans were weaker in the numbers of their defence force than in other African dependencies. Still there were some 200 Europeans, who had all had military training, in addition to native soldiers and police, and they were supplied with machine-guns. They should have put up a much better fight, but they allowed themselves to be rushed. French and British converged on them in five or six small columns, the French from the east and north, the British from the west and, when they had occupied Lome, from the south. Lome, the capital and port of Togoland, is within a mile of the Gold Coast frontier; the German governor did not attempt to defend it, but at once retired up the railway towards the wireless station at Kamina, 100 miles due north of Lome. A detachment of the Gold Coast regiment of the West African Frontier Force occupied Lome on the 7th August 1914, the rest came in on the 12th, and an advance at once began along the road and the railway, which ran parallel to each other. Our fighting men on the main front were only about 600, but in a few days they were joined by 150 French Senegalese from Dahomey. There was one stand-up fight about two-thirds of the way to Kamina, on the 22nd of August. Then the Germans admitted defeat, and surrendered unconditionally on the 26th, first blowing up the wireless station. Though it was itself a small enterprise, it was probably of considerable importance in lowering German prestige among the natives, in setting troops at once free for the Cameroons campaign, and in being a first and successful essay in Franco-British co-operation.

Togoland had an area of 34,000 square miles, rather larger than Ireland. The area of the Cameroons was *The Cameroons.*

over 300,000 square miles, between nine and ten times
as large as Togoland.  One-third of this great territory
had been ceded by France to Germany in 1911, and
the cession included the three tongues of land, which
have been mentioned previously.  The position was
much the same as in Togoland, but on a vastly greater
scale.  The Germans had the French on one side, the
British in Nigeria on the other ; and, where they touched
the Congo, they had the Belgians over against them
on the other bank.  The neutral territory of Spanish
Muni was of much advantage to them ; through it supplies were smuggled in, and into it, at the end, the
Germans who were left escaped.  The Allies were
never able to block it completely.  The enemy's other
advantages were an appreciable and well equipped
fighting force, variously estimated, but probably amount-
ing in all to 1,800 whites and 7,000 native regulars and
police ; the possession of inner lines of communication,
the size of the country, with few roads and fewer
railways to help the invaders, strong natural points of
defence in the north, dense bush in the south, on the
coast a network of creeks and rivers, and in the coast
and forest region a bad climate and heavy rainfall, which
told severely upon the health of the Allied forces,
coloured men as well as white.  The centre of the
Cameroons is a high plateau, the ground slopes down
southwards to the sea and northwards to the valley
of the Benue river and beyond towards Lake Chad.
The western side is much more mountainous than the
eastern.  On the western side in the extreme south
there is the Cameroon mountain, over 13,000 feet high,
and in the far north the isolated Mora group, where
the Germans held out till the end of the campaign.
The main geographical division is between the more

open healthier central and northern region and the
malarious bush and swamp of the south. At the beginning of the campaign, British and French ships
secured the coast-line. The entrance to the Cameroon
estuary and the passage up the estuary on which the
capital Duala stands, were secured, and the main force,
of mixed British and French West African soldiers
under Sir Charles Dobell, fought almost entirely in the
bush region of the south, and at the end of 1914 had
occupied Duala, cleared the two lines of railway, each
of about 100 miles in length, and taken possession of
the Cameroon mountain region, including the mountain
centre of Buea. Small French columns cleared the
before-mentioned tongues of land, and struck at the
centre of the Cameroons. Then, in the first half of
1915, there was an attempt at a converging movement
by these French columns and the main force on Jaunde,
which the Germans had made their centre after losing
Duala, and which stands on the fringe of the forest
belt; but the effort was made too soon, the main force
had to act alone, in insufficient strength, and just as the
rainy season was coming on; eventually it was obliged
to fall back. Subsequently, in the south the rains in
the summer of 1915 held up operations for some months,
and time was given to reorganize and procure rein-
forcements, and also additional equipment from England,
including motor-lorries, which greatly helped the transport. Meanwhile, after somewhat bad reverses at the
very beginning of the campaign, a small Nigerian army,
under General Cunliffe, with a French detachment
added to it, struck at the Germans in the Northern
Cameroons, took the strong position of Garua on the
Benue river over against Yola, and pushed rapidly
south, storming Ngaundere and other mountain strong-

holds. Eventually, as the autumn came on, Cunliffe's
force, in small parallel colums, the French from the
east in small columns, and the main force, in two
columns, on the direct route to Jaunde, all made a converging advance with extraordinary accuracy. Jaunde
was occupied by the main force, and the Germans were
driven over the border into Spanish territory, leaving
only the garrison at Mora, who surrendered when the
fighting was over elsewhere. The campaign ended in
February, 1916, having lasted for a year and a half. Its
great feature was the admirable co-operation between
sailors and soldiers, between French and English, and
between different columns operating at long distances
from each other. It was a very well-managed campaign,
and the West African soldiers showed to great advantage.

*The cam-
paign in
South-
West
Africa.* German South-West Africa was some 320,000 square
miles in area, bordering on British South Africa except
in part of its northern boundary, where it marched
with Portuguese Angola. It was very thinly populated,
a large number of natives having been killed out in the
Herrero war, and the native population, excluding
Ovamboland in the north, and the Caprivi Strip,
did not exceed 80,000 to 90,000, while there were nearly
15,000 whites, mainly Germans, but including an appreciable number of Boer farmers. The coast is wanting
in harbours, much the best harbour belonged to Great
Britain, Walfish Bay, which the Germans took possession of for a short time at the beginning of the campaign. The German ports, such as they were, were
Luderitz Bay in the south, and Swakopmund, about
thirteen miles north of Walfish Bay. The coast region
for some distance inland is a very hot, waterless waste
of sand ; then there is a high plateau running north and
south, where there is much better country, well suited

for European settlement, and then on the inland frontier comes the desert again. The southern boundary was the Orange River. The territory was relatively very well supplied with railways. There were 1,300 miles of line. The railway ran in from the sea at both Luderitz Bay and Swakopmund, and was carried along the plateau north and south, connecting Windhoek, the capital, which had an immense wireless station, with both the ports. From Swakopmund a line also ran away to the north-east mining centres, while in the south the railway was extended south-east to within easy distance of the Cape border.

A large proportion of the German population con-sisted of well-trained reservists. Late in the campaign there were still some 5,000 regulars and reservists in the field. Great stores of guns and military equipment of all kinds, including aeroplanes, had been accumulated, no doubt with the intention of supplying South African rebels. The fighting Union forces numbered at least 50,000, Dutch and British being almost equal in numbers, the mounted troops being mainly Dutch. The great difficulty of the invaders was the desert and the want of water, especially as the Germans poisoned the wells, but Botha, Smuts, and their South African troops were skilled in the kind of warfare required, and their en-veloping movements and bold marches across the desert were such as the Germans did not think possible. They themselves clung to the railways. The British Government was mainly concerned to deprive the Germans of their wireless stations, and the Union Government undertook the campaign. In the latter part of September, 1914, Luderitz Bay was occupied by a force sent round from Capetown. A little later another force, which had been intended to take Swakop-

mund, was, in view of the threatened South African
rebellion, also landed at Luderitz Bay and, except for
pushing inland for a little distance, the forces here
were, in consequence of the rebellion, kept inactive
till the following March.  A third invading force which
was landed at Port Nolloth in the Cape province, and
which crossed the Orange River into the extreme south
of the German protectorate, suffered a severe reverse.
This was partly in consequence of the treachery of the
commandant of the Union troops a little higher up on
the German border, a man named Maritz, who, shortly
afterwards, went into open rebellion.  The rebellion
spread, the former Commandant-General of the Union
forces, Beyers, resigned and joined in it, so did De Wet,
Kemp, and others, but the bulk of the forces remained
loyal.  Botha took the field in person, and, after a
campaign lasting from October to February, the rising
was stamped out, the last fighting being on the German
border, where the Germans supported Maritz.  Meanwhile, Walfish Bay was reoccupied by yet another
force sent round from Capetown, on Christmas Day,
1914, and in the middle of January 1915 Swakopmund
was occupied by the same force.  Swakopmund was
the base for the army under General Botha's personal
command ; General Smuts took the general direction of
the forces operating in the south.  The south was
cleared by columns advancing from south and east
and converging towards the column moving inland
from Luderitz Bay.  One of the columns, under General
Berrangé, made a wonderful march from Kuruman
across the Kalahari desert.  The Luderitz Bay troops
had one hard fight at a place called Gibeon, but by
the end of April the Germans had all been driven
north up the railway, the whole of the southern part

of the Protectorate had been cleared, and a formal Proclamation was issued, taking possession of it. On this land side, railway extension from the Cape Province to German South-West Africa was carried forward at remarkable speed. At the beginning of the campaign the railhead in the Cape in this direction was Prieska; by the 20th November 1914, the railway had been carried from Prieska for 143½ miles to the southern bank of the Orange River over against Upington, and in June 1915, a fortnight before the end of the campaign, it had been taken on for another 173½ miles and linked up to the German railways at Kalkfontein, a temporary bridge being thrown over the Orange River. Meanwhile Botha moved inland from Swakopmund, and in the middle of May took possession of Windhoek, the capital. The Germans, who tried in vain to bargain for terms, retreated along the line of railway to the north-east. They were followed up in June, the mounted burghers, by extraordinary riding through the desert, got round them, and in July they finally surrendered. They were beaten by South African troops and a South African General who thoroughly understood South African warfare. The difficulties were immense, but the horsemen and the motors made their way through the wastes, and upset the enemy's calculations. It was a great triumph of military skill adapted to particular local conditions and of extraordinary endurance by the rank and file. In this campaign, coupled with the rebellion, General Botha and General Smuts, by common consent, showed a combination of military and statesmanlike qualities of the highest order.

German East Africa was the largest of the African *The cam-* possessions of Germany. Its area, population, and main *paign in*

*German
East
Africa.* features have been given in the last chapter. On the northern boundary are high mountains, including Kilimanjaro, the highest in Africa. The largest river is the Rufiji. There is a low-lying coast belt and, except in certain parts, such as the Usumbara mountain region in the north-east, it is an unhealthy region. The opening of the railway from Dâr-es-Salaam to Lake Tanganyika early in 1914 brought a good many German visitors, some of whom were available for fighting when the War came. In the campaign, at one time, Von Lettow Vorbeck seems to have had at his disposal between 3,000 and 4,000 Germans and 15,000 to 20,000 natives. The territory touched on British Protectorates in East Africa, Uganda, Nyasaland, and Northern Rhodesia; it touched on the Belgian Congo in the north-west, and on the south was Portuguese East Africa. Portugal was neutral till March 1916, when she joined the Allies. There was fighting at all points, and on both land and water. On the sea the *Königsberg* gave trouble early in the War, and co-operated in an unsuccessful attack on Mombasa. After she had been finally destroyed up a creek in 1915, the British ships had the coast and the ports more or less at their mercy, but the blockade was not very effective, for two shiploads of arms and munitions reached the Germans. On the great lakes we gained full control of Lake Nyasa by May 1915, and a little later of Lake Victoria and of Lake Tanganyika. On Tanganyika, the Germans had had their own way until Commander Spicer Simson brought two motor-boats out from England, took them overland from the Cape with incredible labour, arrived at the lake at the end of 1915, and disposed of much larger German ships in the early part of 1916. On land we were very weak at the start; especially on

the main front, the boundary of East Africa. There
was fighting on the frontiers of Nyasaland and Northern
Rhodesia, and in the region of Lake Victoria; and on
the main front the Germans occupied Taveta in British
East Africa, which commanded the main entrance into
German territory, raided the Uganda railway, and
threatened Mombasa. Early in November 1914 an
expeditionary force from India was landed near the
German port of Tanga with the view of taking and
occupying it, but made a miserable failure of the
attempt, a full official account of which has never been
published. Then the British were on the defensive more
or less all through 1915. Towards the end of that year
the forces had been strengthened and organized, troops
having come in from South Africa and elsewhere.
General Northey took over command on the Nyasaland side; in the region of Lake Victoria, British and
Belgians prepared for a combined advance; and early
in 1916 General Smuts took over the main command.
He commanded for a year, the Germans were dislodged
from the East African border and by a series of bold
outflanking movements driven perpetually south, until
the whole of the northern part of the protectorate was
cleared, and the main railway seized. Then the line
of the Mgeta river was forced, and then that of the
Rufiji. Meanwhile, in September 1916 Dàr-es-Salaam
was taken by co-operation from the sea. Northey was
advancing too, and the Belgian and Lake Victoria
Forces, Tabora, on the railway, the second town in
the territory, being occupied by the Belgians. The
difficulties of transport were immense, the mortality
and sickness very great, and the white troops were
gradually withdrawn as far as possible. After a year,
General Smuts was succeeded early in 1917 by General

Hoskins, who in turn gave way to another South African General, Van Deventer. As the campaign went south, converging columns moved inland from the sea, from Kilwa and, farther south, from Lindi, Northey's forces and the Belgians co-operated from the inland side, and the main front was always pressing south. Eventually, various bodies of the enemy were caught or surrendered, but Von Lettow and his personal following escaped across the Rovuma river into Portuguese territory. There they replenished their stores from captured Portuguese supplies, evaded pursuit, slipped north again, and, when the armistice came, had just captured the British base of supplies in Northern Rhodesia at Kasama. The campaign lasted the whole of the War, and the German commander was never rounded up. It was an extraordinary feat of endurance and leadership on his part, and it was humiliating that he was never caught, though the whole of his territory had been cleared. It was a very expensive campaign in life and money, and, while making every allowance for the greatest difficulties and admitting that the main object, the conquest and occupation of German East Africa, was achieved, none the less it was the least satisfactory, from the British point of view, of the African campaigns. It ran a course resembling to some extent the later stages of the Boer War, and South African commanders vainly endeavoured to do what British commanders had failed to do in South Africa—to intercept and catch the enemy.

*The Darfur campaign.*    The Sudan has an area of about one million square miles, with some three millions of inhabitants, two-thirds of whom are Moslems. In 1906 a railway had been completed from Atbara junction to the Red Sea

at Port Sudan, giving to the territory an outlet to the
sea, apart from Egypt and over against Jeddah in
Arabia, the port for the pilgrims to Mecca. The entry
of Turkey into the War did not affect the loyalty of
the Sudanese as a whole, with the exception of the
Sultan of Darfur. Darfur is the westernmost province
of the Sudan, and adjoins the French province of
Wadai, and it has an area of over 150,000 square miles,
with a population of under a million. It was the part
of the Sudan most exposed to the Senussi intrigues,
which in turn were fomented by the Turks. In April
1915 the Sultan publicly renounced his allegiance to
the Sudan Government, and later proclaimed a Holy
War, preparing to invade the neighbouring Sudan
province of Kordofan, while the Senussi invaded
Egypt. He had about 10,000 more or less organized
troops armed with modern rifles, in addition to spear-
men and irregular levies. The forces of the Sudan
were some 14,000 men of the Egyptian army, Egyptians
and Sudanese, with a small British garrison at Khartoum. Sir Reginald Wingate, the Governor and Sirdar,
or Commander-in-Chief of the Egyptian army, began
to take action at the end of 1915. The railhead was
El Obeid, 140 miles west of which, within Kordofan
but towards the border of Darfur, was a trade centre
called El Nahud. Here some of the camel corps were
sent in December 1915, and by the middle of March
1916 a small mobile force of 2,000 had concentrated
there. The rains did not begin till July, and the main
difficulty was how to cross the waterless desert; there
were occasional wells at long intervals, but the supplies
of water were largely in hollow trees. As the border
population, however, was growing alarmed and restive,
it was thought necessary to move in the dry season;

with the result that both invaders and defenders were, for want of water, confined to a particular route. The invading force, under Colonel Kelly, moved on in March and April into Darfur, the objective being El Fasher, the capital of Darfur, which is in a direct line more than 300 miles west of El Obeid, and they reached, in the second week of April, a good watering-place, Abiad, about eighty miles east of El Fasher. Here the question again arose whether to wait for the rains in order to attack with overwhelming force, or to strike at once, and it was resolved to move forward, the force being brought up to about 3,000 men and the communications being as far as possible made secure. In the middle of May the advance was made in two columns and another good watering-place was occupied, Melit, over forty miles north by east of El Fasher. Then marching south, through sandhills and scrub towards El Fasher, they came upon the Darfur army about ten miles north of El Fasher; they drew them out of their positions, fought and broke them at close quarters, and next day occupied El Fasher. The Sultan fled and kept up for some time a guerrilla warfare, but was killed in November. It was a very successful little campaign, in the face of great difficulties of both transport and water. Camels and motors were used, but the supply of camels was limited, as so many were at the time required for the armies in Egypt. The French had indirectly co-operated by threatening Darfur from the Wadai side, but the enterprise had all been carried through by native troops under British leadership, with the exception of a small section of British artillery and also of aeroplanes sent up from Egypt, which latter scattered bombs and proclamations. The Sultan had not been popular; Darfur gradually

settled down, and the success, coupled with the keeping
open of the route to Mecca, had a tranquillizing effect
on the peoples of Central Africa, and countered the
Senussi movement.

More or less coinciding with the Darfur expedition *The*
was the fighting with the Senussi on the north coast of *Senussi cam-*
Africa, west of the Delta. The Senussi are called after *paign.*
an African Moslem reformer of that name, who was
born in Algeria and established himself in the middle
of the last century in an oasis in the Libyan desert.
He founded a powerful brotherhood, whose numbers
Lord Cromer estimated at three millions, in different
parts of the Moslem world, but apparently in the past
it was not particularly militant or aggressive, nor did it
always see eye to eye with the Turks. The Senussi
gave no support to the Mahdi in the Sudan. Their
main strongholds were the oases, and on the trade
routes, of the Libyan desert, and the present Senussi
headquarters are in the Kufra oases, due south of
Cyrenaica. They gained special influence in what
became the French province of Wadai, next door to
Darfur. When Turkey entered into the War, the
Turks called on the Senussi, who had co-operated
with them in the Tripolitan campaign, to take up a
Holy War. Through 1915 trouble went on, and at the
end of the year strong action had to be taken. A large
force, including the South African brigade, advanced
west along the north coast of Egypt, and there was
hard fighting, in which the Senussi, led by an Arab
officer of the Ottoman army, were badly beaten.
Sollum, the farthest point on the coast on the Egyptian
frontier, was reoccupied in the middle of March 1916,
motor cars followed up the enemy into the desert,
recovering British prisoners, and the Senussi lost

prestige and power, and gave little further trouble. The success in this fighting must have indirectly contributed to the success in Darfur, which followed immediately afterwards, and the clearing of the western borders of Egypt was a preliminary to the eastward advance in the Sinai Peninsula.

Throughout 1915 and 1916 both France and Spain had much desultory fighting in the western provinces of North Africa, but at no time did any large force coalesce to attack them. The French were also anxious for Tunis up to the date of the British victory over the Senussi. The case of the Italians was more serious.

*The fighting in Tripoli.*
In the course of 1915 all their inland posts in Tripolitania were wrested away, and in 1916 their hold was reduced to little more than the towns and immediate environs of Tripoli and Zuara. Misurata became an open port to Turkish and German submarines, and all to the east of it passed under native control. But the rivalries of the Arab chiefs, and the disinclination of the younger Senussi generation to stand in with the Turks, prevented the total expulsion of the Italians; and in 1917 a change of Senussi policy in favour of Great Britain enabled the latter to bring about an agreement between Mohammed Idris, the new chief of the Senussi, and the Italian representatives in Cyrenaica, under which the former consented to acknowledge Italian suzerainty, if the interior was left to rule itself. The Italians were now able to resume control of the coastline, but they have not even yet re-established their rule to any considerable distance inland.

# XI

## THE RESULT OF THE WAR ON THE MAP OF AFRICA: AFRICAN PROBLEMS

As far as the map of Africa is concerned, the prime results of the War have been the total elimination of Germany from Africa and the total elimination of all Turkish claims and interests in Africa. By the Treaty of Versailles 'Germany renounces in favour of the Principal Allied and Associated Powers all her rights and titles over her Oversea Possessions'. Under the mandatory system created by the Covenant of the League of Nations, which was embodied in this same treaty as an integral part of it and to which further reference will be made, German South-West Africa has passed under the authority of the Union of South Africa; German East Africa has been transferred to Great Britain, with the exception of the north-western areas, the populous sultanates of Ruanda and Urundi, mandated to Belgium; while Togoland and the Cameroons have been divided between France and Great Britain. France has been given the larger part of Togoland, including the capital, Lome, and the railways, and something like nine-tenths of the Cameroons, as the Cameroons stood before the War. It will be remembered that not far short of one-third of the Cameroons, as they stood before the War, had been French prior to 1911.

At the time of the War Turkey had already lost all her territorial possessions in Africa, but she still retained some vested interests. Under the Treaty of Sèvres, she renounced 'all rights and title in or over Egypt', 'all claim to the tribute formerly paid by Egypt', and all rights and privileges in Libya; she recognized in the fullest manner French Protectorate in Morocco and Tunis; and Article 132 laid down that 'outside her frontiers as fixed by the present Treaty, Turkey hereby renounces in favour of the Principal Allied Powers all rights and title which she could claim on any ground over or concerning any territories outside Europe, which are not otherwise disposed of by the present Treaty'.

There are, no doubt, various boundary modifications which have not yet been finally determined, or at any rate not yet given to the public; but, with one possible exception, no less and no more of Africa has been parcelled out among Europeans than before the War. Before the War only Abyssinia and Liberia remained as independent or nominally independent states. They are in the same position still, though apparently the friendly interest of the United States in Liberia is now more exclusive and pronounced than it was. The possible exception is Egypt. The War set it free from Turkish suzerainty and tribute to Turkey and brought it under direct British Protectorate. Now it appears that for British Protectorate is to be substituted a form of modified independence, more independence than the Egyptians have ever previously enjoyed in modern history. The Milner Commission has advocated, in lieu of a Protectorate, a Treaty of Alliance, 'which, while establishing the independence of Egypt, would give to Great Britain all those safeguards and guarantees which the Protectorate, as we understood it, was intended to secure'. The Sudan is not included in the new scheme.

In previous chapters reference has been made to the European dependencies in Africa encircled by other single European powers. France, before the War, encircled one British dependency, the Gambia. She now, as has been seen, also encircles the Gold Coast and Nigeria. She encircles too, as a result of the War, Spanish Guinea, or Muni, in addition to all the other Spanish dependencies in Africa. Before the War Great Britain did not encircle any other European dependency; now, through her mandate for German East Africa, she encircles Portuguese East Africa, and the mandate gives her continuity of territory from the Cape to Egypt.

The exclusion of Germany from Africa has reduced *Result of* by one the number of European nations which control *the elimination of* African lands and peoples. It has removed the Power *Germany* which very specially precipitated and influenced the *from Africa.* scramble for Africa, and it has greatly strengthened the position and added to the territory of some, at any rate, of the Powers which still hold the field in Africa —pre-eminently France and Great Britain. How far is this result likely to benefit Africa, or the reverse? It may be suggested by way of answer that it is clearly for the benefit of Africa that Germany, as Germany was before the War, should have been ousted altogether from the African continent. But it is by no means so clear that Africa stands to gain by a reduction in the number of European nations having holdings and exercising control on African soil. If Germany had been a different kind of nation, her presence in Africa might possibly have been rather an advantage than not to Africa.

This series of studies started by pointing out that *How far* Africa is pre-eminently a dependent or rather *the* *is plurality of* dependent continent, and that it has become in the *European* main a great dependency of Europe. Whether this is *Powers in Africa to*

*the ad-*
*vantage*
*of the*
*Africans?*
good or bad for Africa, it is a fact; the European
Powers which have territorial interests in Africa are
not the least likely to give them up, and if they did,
their exit from Africa at its present stage could only
mean chaos and anarchy. Recognizing, then, this cardinal fact that Africa is a dependency of Europe, how
far is it likely to be to the advantage of Africa that the
nations which bear rule in Africa have been reduced in
number? No one Power, of course, could possibly take
charge of the whole of this vast continent. Much, too,
depends on the character of the colonizing power. It has
been pointed out, for instance, what mischief can come
from the intrusion of a people which has had no training
in the administration of and dealings with native races.
But, assuming that the European peoples are more or less
qualified peoples, the answer to the question, whether
Africa stands to lose or to gain by having fewer or more
European nations taking part in the control of the continent, depends upon the answer to another question,
whether it is more important to give the utmost facilities
for positive work of development or to provide the
greatest possible safeguards against abuse of position
and power? The fewer the controlling Powers are,
the more scope each must have and the larger must be
the areas over which there is the same kind of dealing
and continuity of method. Granted that the intent is
good and the methods moderately wise and just, it must
be more intelligible to native minds and on the whole
more favourable to native interests to deal within well-
defined areas with one and the same type of white man.
This assumes that the political boundaries more or less
correspond with geographical and racial boundaries,
which—largely through ignorance of local topography—
has not always been the case in the past. The boundary

lines, for instance, between the Gold Coast and Togoland, and between Nigeria and the Cameroons, severed native tribes or states. Nor have the anomalies even now been wholly removed. Again, on the face of it, if, by interchange of territory, the spheres of the different Powers could be concentrated outside each other instead of intruding into each other, obvious causes of friction would be removed and the work of development —railway making and the like—would be made easier. If, for example, the French had exclusive control of one great part of Africa and had nothing whatever to do with the rest of the continent, and other Powers similarly, it would seem that there would be more likelihood of assured peace and steady progress.

But there is another and wholly different point of view. *The necessity for mutual checks upon the European Powers in Africa.* Human nature being what it is, the more European peoples there are that have footholds in Africa, the more checks there are upon each individual people. Similarly, the more the spheres of the different European nations are interlaced with each other, the more difficult it is made for any one Power to gain undue predominance. The facts of the late War leave but faint hope that human nature changes materially through the centuries, and it may well be that in the interest of the dependent continent the first and paramount requisite is to provide adequate safeguards against abuse. But the more the power of each European nation in Africa is consolidated, the greater is the possibility of abuse.

In the present posture of affairs lurks a danger both to Africa and from Africa. It is the danger which has been *Africa as a military reservoir.* emphasized by General Smuts, among others, that Africa may be made a military reservoir to serve the purposes of one or other European Power infected (as in the past one nation and another has been at long but compara-

tively regular intervals infected) with the disease of
lust of conquest. That danger alone was a sufficient
reason for turning Germany out of Africa. Her presence
in Africa familiarized Africans with German military
methods, organized them on military lines, and bid fair
to create among them, as among the Germans in Germany, a military caste. The record of Von Lettow
Vorbeck in East Africa showed how formidable an able
German leader could make African fighters and how he
could attach them to his leadership. We have, to our
great advantage, proved the worth of such native African
troops as the Sudanese, the West African Frontier Force,
the King's African Rifles. The French have proved it
still more, as shown by the great number of French
African troops employed in the War. According to
the *Statesman's Year Book*, 92 Senegalese battalions
served, 83 Algerian and Tunisian, and in all 475,000
French native troops, the vast majority of whom were
Africans. When the horrors of war are staled in men's
minds, it may be not only that some European power,
despot or nation, will use African legions to reduce the
world, but also that the Africans themselves may en-
visage their future along military and crusading lines. A
plurality of nations interested in Africa must necessarily
be a safeguard against this danger, as must the presence
of rival Powers in each other's spheres, as for instance
the encircling by France of the British West African
dependencies, and the holding by Great Britain of the
navigable Gambia and the strong position of Sierra
Leone in the midst of French West Africa. This is not
said by way of advocating a dog-in-the-manger policy,
but rather as a reason for not lightly ceding possessions
(some, as the Gambia, of very long standing) in order to
round off the domain of another Power.

The new League of Nations, with the accompanying *The League of Nations.* mandate system[1]—provided that this is not allowed, as the years go on, to become merely a form of words— should be another strong safeguard. In effect the League multiplies the number of non-African civilized nations who are responsible for Africa, and the mandates contain express provisions against the militarizing of the natives in the mandated territories. For instance, the mandate for South-West Africa provides (Article IV): 'The military training of the natives, otherwise than for purposes of internal police and the local defence of the territory, shall be prohibited. Furthermore, no military or naval forces shall be established or fortifications erected in the territory.'

The best side of the scramble for Africa was the adoption, at the Berlin and subsequent conferences, of certain common lines of policy, and the passing of general acts affecting the welfare of the natives in such matters as slavery, liquor traffic, and the like. The Berlin Act, in Professor Keith's words, marked 'a distinct advance in the effort of the nations of Europe to find a common basis of agreement by which to regulate their action in those parts of Africa yet unoccupied, on the basis of freedom of trade and the amelioration of condition of the native races'.[2] However much actual dealings fell short of promises and professions, as in the case of the Belgian Congo, the cause of humanity gained by the common agreement, publicly professed, that certain things ought to be done or ought to be prevented as being consistent or inconsistent with the standard of civilized peoples. The Berlin Act was, *pro tanto*,

[1] See Appendix IV.
[2] *The Belgian Congo and the Berlin Act*, by Arthur Berriedale Keith, D.C.L., D.Litt. (Clarendon Press, 1919), p. 57.

a recognition of the principle of trusteeship. The mandate system carries the principle further. It recognizes that there must be single control over any one area, that a Condominium, such as has been attempted in the New Hebrides, is not a practical working proposition, but it does not admit unfettered ownership of the recovered and mandated areas ; the mandatory Power is placed there in the capacity of managing trustee who has to give a periodical account of his stewardship ; and even assuming that, should occasion arise, the nations who have given the mandate shirk their responsibilities and refuse, in the event of trouble, to intervene, it is still a gain that so much should have been put on paper and stand on record. Even if action is only likely when the mandatory Power is a weak Power, there is still a gain, for weak nations, like weak kings, are rarely good administrators, for the simple reason that they cannot exercise effective control, but they can, without any great upheaval, be coerced. One great outstanding problem of Africa, then, is twofold :—how to prevent its becoming a pawn in the great war game, and how to find safeguards against a possible abuse by the Powers who hold the field in Africa of their position and command of human beings.

So far we have spoken of the problem as, in the main, one for white nations, using the coloured men as their tools, but it must be supposed that, as generations go on, the natives will have a constantly growing voice in the solution or non-solution of these questions. We turn now to the relations between Europeans and natives in Africa generally, and three inquiries suggest themselves : (a) What effect has the War had upon these relations ? (b) What are the main difficulties to be faced in the ordinary tropical parts of Africa ? and (c) What are the

main difficulties—they have been touched upon already
—in those most difficult non-tropical areas, or highland
tropical areas, where the native and the white man dwell
permanently side by side?

The War affected all parts of Africa; it must have *The effect*
made native Africa for the time being either more or less *of the War*
in love with war. But it does not at all follow that the *upon the relations*
Africans have been made more warlike by it. The drain *between*
on the native population, for instance, in Northern *white and coloured.*
Rhodesia and Nyasaland for carrier service in connexion
with the East African campaign, was enormous. It cannot
be supposed that these peoples would like a repetition
of it any more than we should. But, however this may be,
it cannot be doubted that the War tended to equalize
the relations between white and coloured. Natives of
Africa were taken far afield in Africa and, in many
thousands, overseas out of Africa; they saw white men
fighting white men and they were called upon to fight
white men by the side of white men. Their eyes and
minds must have been opened, and they must be asking
questions which never occurred to them before, and
revising their estimates of white men. Incidentally
they have been given more opportunities than could
ever have come to most of them of comparing the kinds
of white men. They will no doubt still follow the
guidance of the white men whom they know and trust,
but it will be a more reasoned following, made cautious
and sophisticated by a knowledge of good and evil.
It has been the same all the world over. The War has
been no respecter of colour and in so far has worked for
racial equality. Its effect in the dependent continent,
in spite of its dependence remaining outwardly as before
the War, must have been profound. What the War has
done brutally and in haste to increase knowledge and

to engender a spirit of equality, missionary effort and education have long been doing in a better way. The tenets of Christianity are radically opposed to discrimination of race, class, or colour; they have for their fundamental basis equality in the sight of God. As Blake puts it:

> My mother bore me in the southern wild
> And I am black, but oh my soul is white.

That these tenets are capable of being applied to racial and political purposes has been shown by disturbing features in the Ethiopian movement among native Christians in South Africa. In Africa we have to face the possibility of millions of natives becoming year by year less unsophisticated and possessed of more race consciousness and more self-respect.

*Problems in the purely tropical regions.* In the tropical lowlands which, so far as can be judged on present data, can never become to any extent homes for Europeans, the sole attraction for the European is the trade in natural or plantation products. In such regions, assuming (as most sensible people will be ready to assume) that European political control cannot, as things are, be dispensed with, the race problem would appear to be twofold. How far is it possible to associate the native in the work of government? How far ought plantations owned by Europeans and worked by native labour to be encouraged or discouraged? An answer to the first of these questions has been supplied by the experience of British dependencies. It has been found good, wherever there is a native organization, a tribe or a sultanate, competent in government, to recognize and support such organization. This practice is valuable because control comes through the native rulers and according to native ways instead of through alien and therefore uncongenial methods. Further, where it has been necessary (either because native organization was non-existent or because it was of such a barbarous nature that it had to be broken up) to create legislative and administrative machinery on European lines, it has been found good to pick out individual Africans of character and education for employ under the Government, and to associate them with the Government by seats in the Legislature.

The question how far white men should be allowed or encouraged to take up plantations in these tropical areas of Africa is more difficult to answer. The extreme proposal has been made that all such white men's plantations in tropical Africa should in future be prohibited. This goes far beyond the sound principle of forming native reserves in the areas where the white and the coloured live and multiply side by side. It is surely an impossible proposal, which, if it were applied to tropical Africa, ought logically to be applied to the tropics of other continents. It is based on the supposition that, because white men's plantations were associated with slavery and oppression of the black man in the past, therefore they will always be a source of abuse ; based again upon the view that it is derogatory for coloured men to work for wages in the employment of white men ; lastly, it rests upon the assumption that the white men have no business in these areas which belong solely to the natives who were in possession when the white men first came. All these contentions are utterly unsound, but the case need not be argued over again. It seems to be forgotten that the white man brings in capital, the latest inventions and machinery, and that a European-owned plantation is an object-lesson and centre of instruction for future native planters. On the other hand, it is beyond question a great move forward when the natives themselves own and cultivate products such as cocoa on the Gold Coast. But native cultivators require to be kept up to the mark. Sir Hugh Clifford, late Governor of the Gold Coast, while noting the phenomenal success of the cocoa industry in that colony, 'almost exclusively in native hands and under native management', pointed out at the same time that cocoa is not an exacting crop, and that the native growers have still to appreciate the value of sustained labour in order to secure good quality in the product. In some parts of the West Indies, where central sugar factories have been built by European plantation owners and merchants, the tendency of later years has been not to use these factories exclusively for sugar-canes grown by native labour on lands belonging to white owners, but to feed them with canes grown by and bought from small native proprietors and cultivators. This seems to be, if the products are not exported in their raw state, a very good method of co-operation between white man and native. Any system that encourages natives to put their hands to permanent as opposed to spasmodic cultivation is to be welcomed. It is better that they should grow products for export rather than content themselves either with growing their daily foodstuffs only, or with gathering forest produce. It is better, again, that they should work for themselves rather than for wages on the white man's lands. But this does not mean that working for European paymasters should be entirely ruled out. How the European capitalist can be eliminated without injuring the native communities into which they have brought their capital is not easy to understand. Human nature is much the same, whether the skin is white or black; cultivators and traders do not cultivate or trade from philanthropic motives, but to make money. Protection of the African need not take the form of discrimination against the European. Lands where white men are few and negligible are not, as a rule, distinguished for industrial or political progress.

Lastly, we come to consider those parts of Africa *The semi-* where white and coloured make homes and rear families *tropical* side by side. We have seen that in North Africa the *ate areas.* coloured races have taken what must be presumed to be more or less final form and shape. They are more or less one with the unchanging East, and the Mohammedan religion has given them a certain cohesion and a definite non-European code of living. The problem here is far easier than where the native races are in the making, because it more or less answers itself; the two races have in a sense agreed to live side by side, but not to fuse and in the main not to compete. Where, on the other hand, Bantus and whites come into juxta-position, as in South Africa, the Bantus are still in the melting-pot and civilization is coming to them in European guise and through Christianity. Every year adds to the number of educated natives, and therefore to the difficulty of the problem. In lands where Europeans cannot live permanently, there cannot be serious competition between black and white, because the whites are few and are birds of passage. In days of slavery there could not be competition, because one race was definitely marked out as masters and owners and the other race as servants; and probably one reason why slavery lasted so long was because, bad as it was, it was simple and intelligible, and coincided with lines of race. The extreme Boer view is not so very far removed from slavery. It is that coloured men should be permanently subordinate to white men.

The traditional British view, on the other hand, is that in principle colour should be no bar to equality. But there is another British view, which has developed with the advent of labour democracy, that coloured labour shall not compete with white labour. In Canada and Australia, where the indigenous coloured men are negligible in numbers, labour is simply concerned to prevent the influx of coloured workers from outside, but in South Africa white labour would like to confine native labour to unskilled work, whereas the mission schools and institutions continue to teach the equalizing doctrines of Christianity and to give industrial training in handicrafts. A reference to the report of the South African Native Affairs Commission, of which Sir Godfrey Lagden was Chairman, and which was published in 1905, shows that the Commission recommended the admission of natives to Parliament, such natives to be elected by native votes alone. This is the principle which has proved so successful in New Zealand, the native members being only a very small minority; but the Union Act of 1909 confines membership of the Union Parliament to British subjects of European descent. Before the Act, in the Legislature of the Cape Colony, natives, if otherwise qualified, were not debarred from a seat because of colour, though as a matter of fact they never sat: now they are definitely debarred from sitting, though not in this particular province of the Union from voting. Thus, with more democracy for the white man, the native cause has politically gone backward not forward. Again, a majority of the South African Native Affairs Commission advocated special encouragement and support to efficient industrial training for natives, but white labour tends to be antagonistic, so far as higher industrial training is concerned.

It is impossible to see what solution can be found for the difficulty or what will be the outcome. All that can be said is that we cannot substantially go back, and most certainly ought not to go back if we could. If you once give self-government, you cannot set limits to self-government. If you give freedom and education and the Christian religion to coloured men, you cannot confine them to a future of permanent subordination. It would be humanly impossible to gather all the natives into some areas and all the whites into others, but the districts which are admittedly native areas should be rigidly kept for the natives, and it is to be hoped that the native territories which are now outside the Union and under the direct control of the Imperial Government will remain as they are, until some adequate political representation is given to natives in the Union Parliament.

If we consider the African races, or at any rate the negro and Bantu races, whether in Africa or in America, their outstanding features are, on the one hand their strength and vitality, and on the other their inability to do without European guidance. What has Hayti or even Liberia made of self-government? The right view of Africa and the Africans is not to regret that Europeans came in, but to deplore that, having come in, they were guilty of so many abuses instead of shouldering their rightful job, which is to be trustees of the black men until in some distant future (if ever) the black men have become able to stand by themselves.

# APPENDIX I

## THE TENURES OF THE EMPIRE

DIFFERENT parts of the British Empire are held by different titles, of which the following list is a summary, though the titles constantly overlap each other.

(a) *Tenure by occupation and settlement,* as e. g. the tenure of *Australia.* It may be argued that, wherever there are native inhabitants, however few, the tenure is not one of settlement but of conquest or of free cession. But *Barbados* and *Bermuda* are instances of colonies which were wholly uninhabited when British occupation began. *Newfoundland,* the oldest British oversea possession, is British in virtue of Sir Humphrey Gilbert's declaration of British sovereignty in 1583 and of later occupation and settlement, but also, as against competing occupiers, the French, in virtue of conquest and treaty of cession—the Treaty of Utrecht in 1713.

(b) *Tenure by conquest*—either

(i) *over another European Power*—such is the British title to *Eastern Canada, Jamaica, Mauritius, Gibraltar;* or

(ii) *over natives,* as in the case of *Burma, Punjab, Ashanti, Zululand,* and others.

(c) *Tenure by free cession.* In this category may be placed, among others, *Malta, New Zealand, Fiji, Basutoland.* The cessions have been made in order to obtain the protection of the British Government either against other European Powers or against unlicensed interlopers, British or foreign.

(d) *Tenure by purchase or lease.* Such was the original title to the site of the city of *Madras. Penang* and *Province Wellesley* were acquired by paying an annuity, still paid, to the Sultan of *Kedah. Sierra Leone* was a case of purchase or nominal purchase. It is a question whether the *Cape Colony* should not be considered rather as a purchase than a conquest. By the post-War arrangement of 1814, Great Britain, in effect, paid £6,000,000 to the

Netherlands for the *Cape* and *British Guiana*. *Cyprus* was occupied on condition of paying an annual sum to Turkey, which was cancelled by the late War. The extension of the colony of *Hong Kong* in 1898 was leased from China for ninety-nine years. *Wei-hai-wei* was leased from China in the same year. The terms of the leases vary, and, as noted in the text, the lease of the landing-place at Chinde, at the mouth of the Zambesi, is not strictly speaking an international lease at all, but is on the footing of a private lease.

(e) *Joint tenure with another Power.* Such is the Franco-British condominium in the *New Hebrides*, and at present the British Egyptian tenure of the *Sudan*.

(f) *Tenure by Protectorate*, which also includes (e). This is strictly speaking not a tenure at all, as the soil of a British Protectorate is not British soil, and the inhabitants are not British subjects. But it is a most important feature of the Empire, including, e. g. *The Feudatory States of India*, the *Malay States*, the *Rhodesias*, and other *South African Protectorates*, nearly the whole of *Nigeria*, &c. (See Appendix II.)

(g) *Tenure by Mandate.* Such is the tenure of *South-West Africa*, *Tanganyika*, &c. This is avowedly a trustee tenure, an outcome of the late War. (See Appendix IV.)

It should be noted that there are many instances of refusal by the British Government to annex or declare a Protectorate when invited to do so. *Fiji* was declined before it was finally accepted. Prior to the scramble for Africa, the mainland coast of the *Sultan of Zanzibar's* territory was offered and refused.

There are instances also of territory which has been surrendered by the British Government, without a *quid pro quo*, as for example the *Ionian Islands* and the *Bay Islands* off the coast of Central America; thus Adam Smith's dictum that ' No nation ever voluntarily gave up the dominion of any province ', is not wholly true.

# APPENDIX II

## THE MEANING OF PROTECTORATE[1]

I. In a speech of July 21st, 1917, the Prime Minister said,
Belgium must be a free people, and not a Protectorate', imply-
ing, what is actually the truth, that a Protectorate is a country
whose freedom is restricted. Similarly the Milner Commission
reported that 'The word "Protectorate" had become a symbol of
servitude in the minds of the Egyptians'.

II. In the British Empire the difference between a Crown
Colony and a Protectorate is that the soil of a Crown Colony is
British soil, and the inhabitants of a Crown Colony are British
subjects, whereas the soil of a Protectorate is not British soil, and
its inhabitants are not British subjects. Thus the Straits Settlements are a Crown Colony, the soil is British soil, and the
inhabitants, white or coloured, other than immigrant aliens, are
British subjects. But in the adjoining Protected Malay States
the soil is not British soil, and the permanent inhabitants are not
British subjects, but the subjects of the Sultans of the respective
States.

III. The above, strictly speaking, holds good both in law and
in fact, but the Protectorates in the British Empire differ very
greatly in kind and in the actual degree of control which is
exercised by the British Government. Thus in Borneo the State
of North Borneo and the State of Sarawak are Protectorates only
in the sense of being under British protection, no more and no
less. The British Government guarantees their security against
foreign enemies, and in turn controls their foreign relations, but it
interferes in no way whatever with their internal administration,
which is wholly in the hands of a chartered company in the one
case, the British North Borneo Company, and of a private
Englishman, Rajah Brooke, in the other. On the other hand, in

---

[1] Reprinted in the main from *History*, January 1918, with the
permission of the Editorial Board.

the Protected Malay States the administration is entirely controlled by the British Residents, who are nominally the advisers
of the Sultans; and, prior to its annexation under the title of the
Kenya Colony, the so-called East Africa Protectorate was to all
intents and purposes a Crown Colony.

IV. The term High Commissioner has very generally been
used in relation to Protectorates to denote the highest authority
on or near the spot. Thus, while the Ionian Islands were under
Great Britain, the British Governor was called High Commissioner, as the islands had not been annexed by Great Britain, but
placed under the protection of Great Britain. Similarly, in the
case of Cyprus the Governor was called High Commissioner,
the island not having been originally annexed, but only occupied
and administered by Great Britain.[1]

V. British Protectorates very commonly adjoin or are neighbouring to British Colonies, and the Governors of the Colonies
are commonly High Commissioners of the neighbouring Protectorates. Thus the Governor of the Straits Settlements is High
Commissioner for the Malay Protectorates; the Governor-General
of the Union of South Africa is High Commissioner for the
South African Protectorates; the Governor of Fiji is High Commissioner for the Protectorates of the Western Pacific.

VI. On the West Coast of Africa—owing to the fact of the
slave-trade which made the original European possessions on
the coast of the nature of forts and factories—the British possessions till quite modern times were far more Protectorate than
Colony (*Hist. Geog. of the British Colonies*, vol. iii, West Africa,
1913 ed., pp. 312–13); and at the present day, though much
annexation has taken place, there is a very great deal of Protectorate, as e. g. at the Gambia (p. 269); and in some cases the
Legislature of the Colony is empowered to legislate for the
Protectorate, and the Protectorate and Colony are more or less
administered together (pp. 275–7). (See also above, pp. 155–6.)

VII. The scramble for Africa, from about 1884–91 more
especially, brought into prominence a very rudimentary form
of Protectorate, called 'Sphere of Influence', meaning that

---

[1] For the term High Commissioner, see *Lord Durham's Report*,
1912 ed., vol. ii, text pp. 7–8 note.

within given limits a certain European Power would be free from interference by such European Powers as agreed to recognize it. In connexion with these Spheres of Influence and with the African Protectorates in their earlier stages the Foreign Jurisdiction Act played a great part. (See Appendix III.)

# APPENDIX III

## CAPITULATIONS AND EXTRA-TERRITORIAL PRIVILEGES

'*CAPITULATIONS*' means simply headings, the headings of Articles, it may be of terms of surrender or of other Agreements. One special meaning of the word denotes the Articles by which the Sultans of Turkey gave special immunities and privileges to the subjects of European nations, when residing within the Turkish dominions. The French obtained such privileges in 1536, and the British Levant Company obtained them in 1583. They were concessions making it worth while for Europeans to live and trade in the Ottoman dominions. They were originally made, as a matter of grace, by a very powerful sovereign, and in *Modern Egypt*, Lord Cromer points out that at first they hardly amounted to treaties, because, in theory, the Moslems were in a state of perpetual war with the Infidels; but they developed into most valuable and most onerous treaty rights, and in Egypt were enlarged by the rulers of Egypt beyond the limits placed to them elsewhere in the Turkish Empire, and became a greater burden and abuse than in any other country.

These Capitulations were what are called *exterritorial* or *extra-territorial privileges*. *Exterritoriality* is defined in the *New English Dictionary* as ' *the condition of being considered outside the territory of the state in which a person resides and therefore of not being amenable to its laws*'. Such is the status of an Ambassador. The French Ambassador in England is not amenable to the laws of England, and the French Embassy in London is, technically, French soil.

This of course is an extreme case, a case of complete exterri-toriality, recognized by the comity of nations.  Among civilized nations, according to the standard of modern civilization, the law for ordinary individuals runs with the soil, and foreigners who go into a country have to obey the law of the land no less than the citizens of the land.  But it was not so to the same extent among European peoples before the nations of to-day were fully organized and standardized, and it is not so to-day in countries which are not so advanced as the alleged civilized nations.  The upward march of a people is marked by the cancelling of exterritorial rights and making foreigners wholly amenable to the law of the land, as, for instance, has been done in Japan.

In the Middle Ages, groups of foreign traders were allowed within limits to form little more or less self-governing communities in the countries of Western Europe, and were only partially amenable to the law of the land.  Such was the status of the Hanseatic Merchants in London, and of the English Merchant Adventurers in the cities of the Low Countries and at Hamburg. The Merchant Adventurers formed, to a limited extent, an *imperium in imperio*.  They were given permission by the rulers of the cities or countries where they sojourned and traded to make their own rules and laws within their own circle and were empowered by their own king to do so.

Before the Turks took Constantinople, the Byzantine Emperors had given exterritorial privileges there to various peoples, especially the Venetians and Genoese, and these rights the Turks renewed. Then the Western nations came on the scene.  It is obvious that when European Christians came into the Turkish Empire they came into conditions, religious, political, social, which were wholly inapplicable to themselves.  There were different standards of justice and of right and wrong.  Polygamy, for instance, is recognized by Mohammedans, it is a crime for Christians.  Ex-territorial privileges and immunities were essential if the incomers were to continue to live as Europeans and Christians, and accordingly such privileges were granted by the Porte.

So far as the British residents in Turkey enjoyed these privileges and were self-governing, they governed and judged themselves through consular officers who were appointed and paid by the Levant Company.  In the year 1825 that Company was dissolved by Act of Parliament, and that Act provided that '*all such rights and duties of jurisdiction and authority*' over British subjects in the ports of the Levant, as had been '*lawfully exercised and performed*' by the consuls or other officers appointed by the Company, should be transferred to Consuls and other officers appointed by the Crown. Thus the enjoyment of exterritorial privileges by British subjects in the Turkish Empire was brought directly under the supervision of the British Government, and in 1836 an Act was passed '*to enable His Majesty to make regulations for the better defining and establishing the powers and jurisdiction of His Majesty's consuls in the Ottoman Dominions*'.

In 1843, by which date we had forced the Chinese to open certain ports, known as *Treaty Ports*, to European trade, a much more far-reaching Act was passed, dealing with the control of British subjects wherever they enjoyed exterritorial privileges. This was the Foreign Jurisdiction Act. It was a law of general application, framed to get over the difficulty of British subjects who lived outside British rule and jurisdiction, and yet not, in whole or part, inside the jurisdiction of the country in which they were living. The preamble of the Act recited that '*by treaty, capitulation, grant, usage, sufferance, and other lawful means, Her Majesty hath power and jurisdiction within divers countries and places out of Her Majesty's Dominions*'. Under this Act authority and jurisdiction has been exercised over British subjects in various Eastern countries, as well as Turkey, notably Siam, China, and, at one time, Japan.

But this Act did not legislate for more barbarous countries, where there was no semi-civilized government to grant these exterritorial privileges, and the difficulty of dealing with British subjects in these countries was accentuated by the scramble for Africa. Consequently, in 1890, the Act of 1843 was replaced by another Act which added a provision that '*where a foreign country is not subject to any government from whom Her Majesty the Queen might obtain jurisdiction in the manner recited by this Act, Her Majesty shall by virtue of this Act have jurisdiction over Her Majesty's subjects for the time being residing in or resorting to the country*'.

This provision was designed to keep order among British subjects in barbarous territories ; but, inasmuch as it was practically impossible to keep order among the white men without keeping order among the natives with whom the white men were in daily contact, the Act was in effect the machinery of a Protectorate, and provided the authority for governing the countries, although they were not British soil.

It will be noted how very British in character has been the evolution of this question; it has gradually adapted itself to time and place, and, as usual, the chartered company, in this case the Levant Company, has figured largely.[1]

# APPENDIX IV

## MANDATES

THE Covenant of the League of Nations, which was incorporated in and formed an integral part of the Treaty of Versailles, provided (Article 22) that

'To those colonies and territories which, as a consequence of the late War, have ceased to be under the sovereignty of the States which formerly governed them, and which are inhabited by peoples not yet able to stand ·by themselves under the strenuous conditions of the modern world, there should be applied the principle that the well-being and development of such peoples form a sacred trust of civilization and that securities for the performance of this trust should be embodied in this Covenant. The best method of giving practical effect to this principle is that the tutelage of such peoples should be entrusted to advanced nations who, by reason of their resources, their experience, or their geographical position, can best undertake this responsibility, and who are willing to accept it, and that this tutelage should be exercised by them as Mandatories on behalf of the League.'

[1] For what has been stated above, see *The Beginnings of English Overseas Enterprise* (Lucas), Oxford University Press, 1917, pp. 151-3, and Sir Albert Gray's note on page xliii of the Introduction to *Early Voyages and Travels in the Levant* (Hakluyt Society Series, 1893).

It was laid down that the character of the Mandate must differ in different cases, e. g. that certain communities formerly included in the Turkish Empire could be provisionally recognized as independent nations, 'subject to the rendering of administrative advice and assistance by a mandatory until such time as they are able to stand alone'; and that, for other peoples, especially in Central Africa, the mandatory must be responsible for the administration, under conditions guaranteeing freedom of religion, prohibition of slave-trade, arms, and liquor traffic, prohibition of 'the establishment of fortifications or military and naval bases and of military training of the natives for other than police purposes and the defence of the territory'. The Mandate also assured guarantees for freedom of trade for all members of the League, and asserted that some territories 'such as South-West Africa and certain of the South Pacific Islands', for various reasons, 'can be best administered under the laws of the mandatory as integral portions of its territory', subject to the safeguards already mentioned.

Annual reports were to be rendered to the Council of the League of Nations by the various Mandatories, and a Permanent Commission was to be constituted to examine the reports and advise the Council upon them.

Thus tenure by Mandate is a definitively trustee tenure, and the Mandatory Power is a managing trustee, bound over to give an account of its stewardship year by year.

# APPENDIX V

## NOTE ON BOOKS

STANDARD works on all parts of Africa are numerous and constantly multiplying. This note is intended for teachers and others who only want either shorter or more general books. The *Peace Series* of handbooks, prepared under the direction of the Historical Section of the Foreign Office, and published by H.M. Stationery Office, 1920, gives most careful and accurate accounts of various sections of Africa in all their phases, together with full bibliographies. The articles in the *Encyclopædia Britannica*, up to the date of the last edition, 1911, are full of information by first-rate authorities, and also give bibliographies which can be supplemented from the *Statesman's Year Book*. For the British Colonies and Dependencies in Africa the annual *Colonial Office List* should always be consulted. Up to 1895, the date of the 2nd edition, Sir John Scott Keltie's *Partition of Africa* (Edward Stanford) is most valuable. Sir Harry Johnston, as a first-hand authority on Africa, is second to none, and among his short text-books are *A History of the Colonization of Africa by Alien Races* (Cambridge Historical Series, 1889), and *The Opening-up of Africa*, in the Home University Library (Williams and Norgate, 1911). On the Belgian Congo, &c., Professor Keith's *The Belgian Congo and the Berlin Act* has been already quoted in the text. For the German connexion with Africa, Mr. Evans Lewin's *The Germans and Africa* (Cassell & Co., 1915) should be used; and a good very short summary of the campaigns against the Germans in Africa is contained in Mr. H. C. O'Neil's *The War in Africa and in the Far East* (Longmans, Green & Co., 1919). Mention should also be made of *The Oxford Survey of the British Empire*, vol. iii, *Africa* (Clarendon Press, 1914); of Mr. Wyatt Tilby's *English People Overseas*, vol. iv; *Britain in the Tropics* (Constable & Co., 1912); and of the West African and South African volumes of *The Historical Geography of the Colonies* (Clarendon Press, 1913–15). Finally, the year 1922 has produced a book on tropical Africa of first-rate importance in Sir Frederick Lugard's *The Dual Mandate in British Tropical Africa* (William Blackwood & Sons).

# INDEX

Abd-el-Kader, 64, 124.
Abiad, 190.
Abyssinia, 11, 26, 27, 58, 90, 96, 102, 110, 116; boundary agreements, 102; independence, 102, 194.
Abyssinians, 30.
Accra, 39.
Aden, 63, 89.
Adowa, battle of, 102.
African Association (1788), 58.
Agades, 177.
Agadir, 107.
Albany Settlement, 138.
Albert, King of the Belgians, 85.
Albert Edward, Lake, 83, 101.
Albert Nyanza, 68, 69.
Albreda, 60.
Alexander the Great, 18.
Alexandria, 18.
Algeciras Conference (1906), General Act of the, 106.
Algeria, 12, 23, 24, 27, 30, 63-4, 79, 117, 119-21, 150; French occupation, 122-7.
— Northern, 125, 126.
— Southern, 126.
Algerian pirates, 121, 127.
— troops, 198.
Algiers, 63, 64, 77.
Algoa Bay, 34.
Ama Xosa Bantus, 140.
Ambas Bay, 62, 94.
Ambriz, 81.
America and the slave-trade, 42-4, 52, 56-7, 162.
American Colonization Society, 56.
Amiens, Peace of, 137.
Anglo-Dutch Convention (1871), 61-2.
Anglo-French Agreement (1857), 60; (1890), 95; (1899), 101;

Convention (1904), 103-4, 106, 153.
Anglo-German Treaty (1890), 91-3, 95, 104, 109; Agreement (1893), 101.
Anglo-Portuguese Treaty (1884), 81-2, 92, 106; (1891), 113, 115.
Angola, 14, 29, 35, 38, 41, 44, 71, 77, 81, 182.
Annobon, 41.
Arab conquest of North Africa, 26-8.
Arabi Pasha, 130.
Arabia, 166.
Arabs, 30, 34, 35, 37, 39, 73, 124, 170, 192; and the slave-trade, 42, 71.
Arguin, Bay of, 35.
— island of, 13.
Arnold, Dr. Thomas, 21.
Arnold, T. W., 22.
Ascension, 40, 41.
Ashanti, 151, 156, 157.
Asiatic immigration, 31, 117, 119, 120, 122, 163-4, 175.
Assab, 89.
— Bay, 79, 89.
Assinie, 36, 61, 62.
Asturias, 32.
Atbara, 115, 188.
Atlas Mountains, 113.
Austrian Company, 39.
Azores, 33, 41.

Bagamoyo, 166.
Baker, Sir Samuel, 68.
Bangweolo, Lake, 69.
Bantus, 30, 31, 140, 141, 147, 170, 205, 207.
Baptist missionaries, 62, 94, 165.
Barbados, 43.
Barbary pirates, 63, 64.
Barca, 127.

Barruwa, 95.
Barth, Dr., 65.
Basutoland, 63, 142, 143, 148.
Bathurst, 60, 61.
Bathurst, Lord, 60.
Beaconsfield, Lord, 64, 87.
Beazley, C. R., 27.
Bechuanaland, 67, 93.
— British Protectorate, 67, 93.
Bechuanas, 30, 74.
Beira, 15, 115.
— railway, 113.
Belgian Congo, 49, 79, 84–6, 109, 111, 112, 115, 116, 199; atrocities, 85–6, 98, 172. *See also* Congo Independent State.
Belgian railways, 115.
Belgium and Africa:
Congo, the, 84–6, 97.
East Africa, 164, 168, 193; campaign in, 178, 180, 187, 188.
*See also* Belgian Congo *and* Congo Independent State.
Benadir Coast, 90.
Benguela railway, 14, 116.
Benin, 151.
Benue river, 95, 112, 180, 181.
Berbers, 30.
Berlin Conference (1885), General Act of the, 82–3, 86, 88, 106, 199.
Berrangé, General, 184.
Beyers, General, 184.
Biafra, Bight of, 62.
Bismarck, Prince, 78, 88.
Blantyre, 68, 115.
Boers, 63, 74, 77, 102, 119, 136, 138–49, 170, 176, 182, 205.
Bonn, Prof. Moritz, 169.
Bornu, Sultanate of, 65.
Botha, General, 177, 183–5
Botha, Graham, 136.
Bourbon, or Réunion, 40, 41.
Brandenburgers in West Africa, 39.
Brazzaville, 153.
Breda, Peace of, 38.
British Bechuanaland Protectorate, 143.
British East Africa Protectorate, 16, 102, 165, 169, 170; campaign in, 187. *See* Kenya Colony.

British Levant Company, 213–16.
British Somaliland Protectorate, 26, 89, 90.
British South Africa Company, 93, 98.
British West Indies regiment, 178.
Bruce, James, African explorer, 58.
Brussels Conference (1889–90), General Act of the, 83.
Bryce, Lord, 21.
Buea, 161, 181.
Bukama, 115.
Buluwayo, 115.
Burton, Richard, 68.
Bushmen, 29, 30, 31, 139.
Bussa, 65.

Cadiz, 19.
Caillé, French explorer, 65.
Calicut, 34 and *n*.
Cambon, M. Jules, 23–4, 26, 27, 117, 120, 123, 124, 150.
Cameron, Lovett, 69–70.
Cameroon Coast, 62.
— Estuary, 14.
— mountain region, 157, 161, 163, 180, 181.
Cameroons, the, 13, 88, 94, 95, 101, 103, 107–9, 111, 112, 152, 153, 161, 165, 193, 197; campaign in, 177–82.
Canary Islands, 13, 33, 35, 37, 41, 108.
Cape Agulhas, 34.
Cape Blanco, 34, 96, 108.
Cape Bojador, 33, 34, 96.
Cape Colony (now Cape Province), 63, 74–5, 88, 135–49, 184, 185, 206, 209–10.
Cape Delgado, 34, 77, 166.
Cape Guardafui, 34.
Cape Juby, 96.
Cape Mesurado (or Montserrado), 56.
Cape of Good Hope, 15, 33–5, 38–41, 63, 64.
Cape Palmas, 34, 57, 61.
Cape to Cairo railway, 101, 116.
Capetown, 115, 136, 183, 184.
Cape Verde, 34, 36.
— — islands, 33, 41.

Cape Voltas, 34.
Capitalism, 29, 151-2, 174, 203-5.
Capitulations and extra-territorial privileges, 131-2, 213-16.
Caprivi Strip, 67, 93, 109, 112, 182.
Carthage, 19, 20, 25.
Carthaginians, 17, 19, 20, 21.
Casablanca, 106, 107.
Central Africa, 67-71, 86, 217.
Ceuta, 32, 33, 41, 64, 108, 113.
Chad, Lake, 65, 66, 95, 103, 112, 180.
Chaka, Zulu chief, 31, 140.
Chambezi river, 69.
Chartered Companies, 98-9.
Chinde, 115, 210.
— channel, 16.
Chindio, 115.
Chinese labour, 173.
Chirol, Sir Valentine, 128, 130.
Chobe river, 67.
Christianity, 27, 28, 32, 72, 121, 123, 130, 165, 202, 205, 207, 214. *See also* Missionaries.
Christiansborg Castle, 37.
Clapperton, Hugh, 65.
Clifford, Sir Hugh, 15 *n.*, 159-61, 176, 204.
Comité des Études du Haut Congo, 80.
Congo Independent State, 83-4, 93, 97, 101, 151. *See also* Belgian Congo.
Congo International Association, 80, 81, 82, 83.
Congo river, 14, 33, 38, 58, 65, 69-71, 77, 80-3, 93, 109-15, 153, 180.
Corisco Bay, 62.
Cory, Professor, 141.
Crete, 20.
Cromer, Lord, 85, 98, 100, 126, 128, 129, 131, 132, 191, 213.
Cunha, Tristan da, 40.
Cunliffe, General, 181, 182.
Cyrenaica, 19, 110, 127, 191, 192.
Cyrene, 19.

Dahomey, 96, 103, 151, 179.
Dakar, 153.
Danes in West Africa, 37, 39, 41, 61, 62.

Dâr-es-Salaam, 15, 69, 165, 186, 187.
— to Tanganyika railway, 116.
Darfur, 101, 177, 189-92 ; campaign in, 188-91.
— Sultan of, 177, 189.
de Brazza, Savorgnan, 80, 81.
Delagoa Bay, 15, 39, 63, 77.
Delarey, General, 144.
Delcassé, M., 106.
De Wet, General, 184.
de Winton, Sir Francis, 80.
Diamond Fields, 63, 147.
Diaz, Bartholomew, 33, 136.
Dobell, Sir Charles, 181.
Drakensberg Mountains, 113.
Duala, 14, 181.
Du Bois, W. E. B., 56.
Durban, 113, 142.
D'Urban, Sir Benjamin, 141.
Dutch and South Africa, 39-40, 74, 112, 120, 135-49. *See* Boers.
— and West Africa, 36-9, 41, 61, 62.
— and the slave-trade, 44-6.
— troops in the World War, 183-5.
Dutch Reformed Church, 145.

East Africa, 15, 16, 90-3, 163-75. *See also* British, German, *and* Portuguese East Africa.
East Indians, 52, 53.
Edward VII, 103.
Egypt, 9, 10, 15-19, 21, 26, 27, 87, 89, 96, 100, 101, 104, 105, 110, 127-30, 166, 172, 177, 189, 190-2 ; British occupation, 131-3, 194 ; independence of, 194.
— Khedive of, 128.
Egyptian army, 189.
— race, 30.
Eliot, Sir Charles, 166, 170, 173-4.
Elmina, castle of, 35, 37.
Emin Pasha relief expedition, 83.
Enclaves, 84, 108, 113.
Eritrea, 89, 102.
Ethiopian movement, 202.
Exmouth, Lord, 64.

Fasher, El, 190.
Fashoda, 100, 103.

Fernando Po, 13, 41, 62.
Ferry, M. Jules, 124.
Forbes, Mrs. Rosita, 191.
Forcados, 14.
Foreign Jurisdiction Act, 213, 215.
France and Africa, 25, 77-9, 87, 88, 91, 97, 159, 160, 197.
Algeria, 63-4, 117, 120-7.
Cameroons, 193.
Congo, 80-4, 94, 100, 107-9.
East Africa, 40, 41, 63, 92, 94.
Egypt, 104, 105.
Equatorial Africa, 94, 107-9, 153.
Madagascar, 92.
Morocco, 104-8, 126, 194.
North Africa, 12, 23, 77, 79, 89, 110, 111, 119-26, 192.
North-East Africa, 89, 90, 92, 110.
Sudan, 100, 101.
Togoland, 193.
Tunis, 126, 133, 194.
West Africa, 14, 35-6, 38, 40, 60-2, 77, 94-6, 103, 104, 113, 152-3, 160, 195, 198.
— and the campaigns in Africa, 178-82, 190; and the slave-trade, 46-7, 49.
— political relations with :
Germany, 94, 105-9, 180.
Great Britain, 95, 97, 100-4, 112, 152-3, 163, 164.
Spain, 102-4, 107, 108.
Franco - German Agreement (1911), 107.
Franco - Spanish Convention (1900), 102-3.
Fransche Hoek, 136.
Freeman, Prof. E. A., 23, 25, 120, 122.
Freetown, 157.
French Congo, 81, 100.
French Equatorial Africa, 94, 107-9, 153.
French native troops, 198.
— railways, 116.
Frere, Sir Bartle, 73, 88, 90, 166.
Fuller, Sir Francis C., 157 *n*.

Gaboon, 94, 153.
— river, 62.
Gama, Vasco da, 18, 34.

Gambia, 96, 111, 113, 153-5, 157, 178, 195, 198, 212.
— river, 14, 33, 35-8, 41, 50, 58, 60, 61, 64, 104, 112.
Garua, 181.
Gaunt, Mrs. Mary, 161.
German East Africa, 15, 16, 69, 88, 91, 92, 101, 111, 114, 164-9, 178, 185-8, 201 ; railways, 116; campaign in, 178, 185-8, 201 ; British mandate for, 193, 195. *See* Tanganyika Territory.
German South-West Africa, 37, 67, 88, 93, 110, 112, 113, 142; campaign in, 177, 182-5; mandate for, given to the Union of South Africa, 193, 199, 210, 217.
Germany and Africa, 25, 78, 79, 82, 86-8, 90, 97, 159, 161-2, 172, 176-7, 198.
Congo State, 82-4.
East Africa : *see* German East Africa.
Morocco, 104-8.
North Africa, 109.
South-West Africa : *see* German South-West Africa.
West Africa, 94-6, 101, 103, 107-9, 111, 152, 161, 177-82, 193. *See also* Cameroons *and* Togoland.
Zanzibar, 92.
— and the campaigns in Africa, 176-83 ; exclusion from the continent, 193, 195.
— political relations with :
France, 94, 105-9, 180.
Great Britain, 94, 95, 97, 101, 112, 166-7.
Portugal, 93.
Gibbon, Edward, 21.
Gibeon, 184.
Gibraltar, 113.
— Straits of, 19, 26.
Gladstone, W. E., 87.
Glasgow Missionary Society, 73, 75.
Glenelg, Lord, 74, 141.
Gold Coast, 14, 17, 35-9, 41, 61, 62, 96, 103, 153-7, 159, 162, 163, 195, 197, 204; troops in the War, 178, 179.
Goldie, Sir George Taubman, 95.

Gondokoro, 68.
Gordon, General, 72.
Goree, island of, 13, 36, 38.
Graaf Reinet, 136.
Grain Coast, 54, 58, 61.
Grant, J. A., 68.
Great Britain and Africa, 18, 22, 29, 32, 53, 65, 67, 76–9, 88, 91, 97, 98, 115, 158–61.
Congo State, 81–4, 112.
East Africa, 63, 70, 71, 91–3, 101, 102, 110, 112, 163–75, 193, 195.
Egypt, 87, 89, 100, 104, 105, 121, 126–7, 131–3, 194.
Morocco, 104–6.
North-East Africa, 89, 90, 110, 192.
South Africa, 39–41, 63, 73–5, 77, 87, 88, 92–3, 102, 112, 120, 136–49, 209.
Sudan, 100, 101, 210.
Suez Canal, 64.
West Africa, 36, 38, 41, 60–2, 77, 93–6, 103, 111, 113, 152–64, 193, 195, 198, 212.
See also under the several dependencies.
— and the campaigns in Africa, 176–92; and the slave-trade, 44–52, 71, 81.
— political relations with :
France, 95, 97, 100–4, 112, 152–3, 163, 164.
Germany, 94, 95, 97, 101, 112, 166–7.
Portugal, 92, 93, 95, 106, 113, 115, 195.
Great Fish river, 140.
Greek colonies, ancient, 19.
Grey, Sir Edward, 85.
Griqualand West, 63.
Guinea coast, 36, 45, 62 n.
— Gulf of, 33, 39, 95, 103.

Hamites, 30.
Hannibal, 20.
Hannington, Bishop, 165.
Harbours, 13–15, 165, 182.
Hawkins, Sir John, 36, 45.
Hawkins, William, 36, 45–6.
Hedjaz (Arabia), 26.
Heligoland, cession of, 92, 104.
Henry the Navigator, Prince, 33.

Herrero war, 182.
High Commissioner, the term, 212.
Hispaniola, 44, 45, 46.
Horn of Africa, 26, 90.
Hoskins, General, 188.
Hottentots, 29, 31, 139, 140.
Huguenot immigration, 136.

Ifni enclave, 108.
Île de France : see Mauritius.
Imperial British East Africa Company, 90, 91, 98, 102, 165.
India, 89–91, 164.
Indian immigration, 31, 175.
— traders, 174.
— troops in the African campaigns, 178, 187.
Indian Ocean, 116.
International African Association, 79, 80.
Isles de Los, 104.
Ismail, Khedive, 129, 130.
Italian Somaliland, 90, 102, 164.
Italy and Africa, 78, 79, 87, 97.
Abyssinia, 90, 96, 102.
North Africa, 79, 110, 192.
North-East Africa, 90, 110.
Red Sea coast, 89, 90.
Somaliland, 90, 102, 164.
Tripoli, 109–10, 127.
Tunis, 126.
— war with Turkey, 109–10, 127.
Ivory Coast, 36, 61, 62, 96, 103.

James I, 39.
Jaunde, 181, 182.
Jews in North Africa, 121.
Johnson, Dr., and the slave-trade, 48, 51.
Johnston, Sir Harry, 29, 126.
Juba river, 16, 90, 110.

Kabinda, 81, 93, 94, 110.
Kaffirland, 138, 140.
Kaffirs, 30, 74, 139–41.
Kalahari desert, 184.
Kalkfontein, 185.
Kamina, wireless station at, 176, 179.
Kano, 115, 165.
Kasama, 188.
Katanga, 116.
Kei river, 140.

Keith, Prof. A. Berriedale, 199.
Kelly, Colonel, 190.
Kemp, General, 184.
Kenya Colony, 150, 162, 163, 167–70, 175. *See* British East Africa Protectorate.
Khartoum, 58, 100.
— railway, 114, 115.
Kigoma, 69, 165.
Kilimanjaro Mountain, 186.
Kilindini, 15, 170.
Kilwa island, 15.
Kilwa Kisiwani, 15.
Kimberley, 147.
King's African Rifles, 165, 178, 198.
Kirk, Sir John, 68, 90.
Kitchener, Lord, 91, 100.
Konakry, 104.
*Königsberg*, the, 186.
Kordofan, 189.
Kosa Bantus, 140.
Kruger, President, 142.
Krumen, or Kruboys, 58.
Kufra oases, 191.
Kuruman, 66, 184.

Lado enclave, 84.
Lagden, Sir Godfrey, 206.
Lagos, 62, 65, 94, 154, 156, 165; British Protectorate, 96.
— to Kano railway, 115.
Laing, Alexander Gordon, 65.
Lakes, 14, 66–71, 111–16, 165, 166.
Lander, John, 65.
Lander, Richard Lemon, 65.
Lansdowne, Lord, 103.
Larache, 108.
Lausanne, Treaty of (1912), 110.
League of Nations, 193, 199, 216–17.
Leopold, King of the Belgians, 79, 80, 83–5.
Lettow Vorbeck, Von, 186, 188, 198.
Liberia, 11, 54, 61, 96, 110, 111, 153, 194, 207; founding of the Republic of, 56–8.
Libya, 177, 194.
Libyan desert, 12, 127, 191.
Lindi, 15.
Livingstone, David, 10, 18, 42, 53, 60, 63, 66–73, 164, 174.

Livingstone Mountains, 68.
Livingstone (town), 67.
Loanda, 67.
Lobito Bay, 14, 116.
Lome, 193.
London Missionary Society, 66, 67, 72–5.
Lualaba river, 69, 70.
Luderitz Bay, 182, 183, 184.
Lugard, Sir Frederick, 159–61.
Lukuga river, 115.
Lyautey, Marshal, 160.

McCarthy's Island, 61.
MacKinnon, Sir William, 91.
Maclean, Capt. George, 155.
MacMahon, Marshal, 63.
Madagascar, 30, 40, 41, 110; French Protectorate, 92.
Madeira, 33, 41.
Mahdi, the, 191.
Makololo tribe, 67.
Malay Peninsula, 53, 159.
Malays at the Cape, 136.
Mandates and mandatory powers, 193, 199, 200, 210, 216–17.
Mansfield, Lord, 54.
Marchand, Major, 100.
Maritz, Commandant, 184
Maryland, 57.
Masai, the, 170–1.
Mashonaland, 92, 93.
Massowah, 89.
Matabele, 147.
Maugham, R. C. F., 56, 57.
Mauritius (Île de France), 31, 40, 41.
Mediterranean, the, 9, 12, 15, 18–20, 25, 31, 63, 108, 119.
Mehemet Ali, 128, 129.
Melilla, 41, 108.
Melinde, 34.
Melit, 190.
Mesopotamia, 18, 19.
Mgeta river, 187.
Mikindani, 15.
Milner, Lord, 113 *n.*, 128, 134, 135, 142.
— Commission, 194, 211.
Missionaries, 62, 63, 68, 72–6, 86, 88, 98, 119, 145, 147, 164, 165 169, 174, 175.
Misurata, 192.
Moero, Lake, 69.

Moffat, Dr. Robert, 66, 73.
Mohammedanism, 13, 17, 23, 26–8, 30, 32, 43, 53, 122, 123, 125, 128, 151, 158, 176, 177, 188, 191, 205, 213, 214.
Mohammed Idris, 192.
Molema, S., 138, 139, 141, 145.
Mombasa, 15, 34, 63, 102, 165, 168, 170, 186, 187.
Monrovia, 56.
Moors, the, 32.
Mora, 180, 182.
Morocco, 17, 26, 27, 30, 37, 41, 96, 104–8, 113, 119, 123, 160; French Protectorate, 107–8, 126, 194.
Mozambique, 15, 35, 38, 41.
Muni, dependency : see Spanish Guinea.
Muni river, 62, 94.
Muscat, 90, 91, 166.
— Sultan of, 166.

Nahud, El, 189.
Nairobi, 167, 169, 170.
Napoleon I, 18, 40.
Napoleon III, 124.
Natal, 35, 53, 63, 137, 142, 169.
National African Company, 94.
Native races and the native question, 28–32, 118, 135, 138–41, 143, 145–52, 155, 157–63, 168, 170–1, 174–5, 196, 199–207.
— labour, 172–3.
— reserves, 171.
— troops, 197–9.
Navigation Acts, 45, 46.
Negroes, 30, 31, 33, 36, 207 ; and the slave-trade, 42–57.
Nero, 22.
Netherlands East India Company, 135–8, 143.
Newfoundland Treaty (1904), 104.
Newton, Rev. John, 51.
Ngami, Lake, 67, 71.
Ngaundere, 181.
Niger Coast Protectorate, 94.
— delta, 62, 65.
Niger river, 14, 36, 38, 58, 64, 65, 69, 82, 94, 95, 103, 112, 165.
— Lower, 112, 116.
— Middle, 112.
— Upper, 112.
Nigeria, 62, 104, 153, 154, 156–9, 161, 163, 197, 210; British Protectorate, 94 ; railway, 115.
Nigeria, Northern, 65, 151, 154, 158–60, 165, 177.
— Southern, 154, 159.
Nigerian troops, 178, 181.
Nile river, 16–18, 22, 68–70, 83, 84, 101, 112, 114, 170.
— Blue, 58.
— Lower, 9.
— Upper, 84, 112, 168.
— White, 58, 100.
Nilotic tribes, 170.
North Africa, 19–24, 117–33, 150, 192, 205.
Northern Territories, 156.
Northey, General, 187, 188.
Nun river : see Wad Draa.
Nyangwe, 70.
Nyasa, Lake, 68, 69, 110, 111, 114, 186.
Nyasaland, 68, 92, 93, 98, 163, 164, 174–5, 187, 201 ; railway, 114–15.

Obeid, El, 189, 190.
Obock, 63, 79, 89.
Ogove river, 33, 63, 80, 94.
Oil Rivers Protectorate, 65, 94.
Omdurman, battle of, 100.
Ophir, 17.
Orange Free State Province, 113, 142.
Orange River, 14, 88, 110, 183–5.
Ottomans : see Turks.
Ovamboland, 182.

Palmerston, Lord, 72.
Palm-oil and kernels, 151–2, 157.
Park, Mungo, 58, 64 65, 69.
Pemba, 92, 164.
— Bay, 15.
Persian Empire, 18.
Philip, Dr. John, 74, 75.
Phoenicians, 17, 19.
Pietermaritzburg, 142.
Plantations, 202–5.
Port Amelia, 15.
Portendik, Bay of, 60.
Port Nolloth, 184.
Port Sudan, 115, 189.
Portugal and Africa, 31–5, 38, 39, 41, 77, 86, 135.

Portugal and Africa *(cont.)* :
Congo, the, 81–3, 93, 97.
East Africa : *see* Portuguese East Africa.
North Africa, 25, 32, 33.
West Africa, 14, 33, 35, 37, 71, 77, 92–3, 95, 96, 111 ; railways, 116. *See also* Angola *and* Portuguese Guinea.
— and the slave-trade, 44, 47, 71 ; and the campaigns in Africa, 178, 186, 188.
— political relations with Great Britain, 92, 93, 95, 106, 113, 115, 195.
Portuguese East Africa, 15, 34, 35, 40, 63, 72, 77, 90, 92–3, 110, 164, 195.
Portuguese Guinea, 37, 41, 77, 95, 96, 111, 113.
Prempeh, king of Ashanti, 157.
Prieska, 185.
Principe, island of, 41, 44.
Protectorates, 210 ; meaning of the term, 211–13.
Ptolemies, the, 19.
Ptolemy, the geographer, 18.

'Queen Adelaide province', 140–1.
Quilimane, 67.

Railways, 113–16, 142, 183, 185, 186, 188, 193.
Red Sea, 17, 18, 26, 63.
— — coast, 11, 89, 90, 116, 131 ; railways, 116, 188–9.
Réunion : *see* Bourbon.
Rhodes, Cecil, 115.
Rhodesia, 145, 169, 178, 210.
— Northern, 67, 69, 93, 134, 143, 187, 188, 201, 210.
— Southern, 15, 18, 93, 143, 210.
Rio del Rey Creek, 94.
Rio de Oro, Spanish Protectorate of, 96, 103, 107, 113.
Ripon Falls, 114.
Rivers, 14, 16, 66–71, 82, 111–16.
Rodrigues, 40, 41.
Roman Empire in Africa, 18–24.
Rovuma river, 68, 69, 92.
Royal Geográphical Society, 58, 69.
Royal Niger Company, 94–5, 98, 154, 165.

Ruanda, Sultanate of, 168, 193.
Rufiji river, 16, 169, 186, 187.
Ryswick, Treaty of, 46.

Sahara, the, 12, 27, 30, 66, 108, 119, 191.
— coast, 96.
St. Helena, 39, 41.
St. John river, 60.
St. Marie, island of, 40.
St. Mary's Island, 60.
St. Thomas, island of, 41, 44.
Saldanha Bay, 14.
Salisbury, Lord, 95.
Sanga river, 109.
Saracens, the, 26, 32.
Say, 95.
'Scramble for Africa', 60, 70, 77 ff.
Segu, 58.
Self-government, 207.
Semites, 30.
Senegal, 35, 36, 38, 41, 112, 153.
— river, 33, 58, 60, 64, 114.
Senegalese, 36, 179.
— troops, 198.
Senegambia, 38, 60, 96 ; railways, 116.
Senussi, the, 127, 177, 189, 191.
— campaign, 191–2.
Septimius Severus, 21.
Sèvres, Treaty of, 193.
Seychelles, 40, 41.
Shiré Highlands, 67–8, 114, 115, 163, 173, 175.
— river, 67, 114.
Sierra Leone, 14, 17, 33, 39, 41, 57, 61, 96, 104, 153–5, 157, 165, 198, 209 ; colony for free negroes at, 53–6.
Simon's Bay, 15.
Simson, Commander Spicer, 186.
Slave Coast, 62, 95, 96, 103.
Slavery and the slave-trade, 17, 30, 31, 33, 39, 42–56, 62, 66, 71, 74, 81–3, 90, 145, 150, 154, 162, 166, 172, 203, 205, 212 ; abolition of, 47–8, 151, 154, 162.
Smith, Adam, 46, 49.
Smuts, General, 183–5, 187, 197.
Socotra, island of, 89.
Sokoto, Sultanate of, 65.
Sollum, 191.
Somali coast, 63.

Somaliland, 26, 89, 90, 102, 164, 165.
Somalis, 30, 170.
South Africa, 63, 92-3, 119, 120, 134-49; conquest and settlement, 135-40, 146-9; Great Trek, the, 74, 141; Kaffir wars, 140-1; mission-fields, 73-5; natives, 29-31, 143, 145-9, 205-7; rebellion during the War, 177, 183, 184; troops in the late campaigns, 177, 178, 183-5, 187-8, 191.
South Africa, Union of, 10, 50, 119, 143-5, 183, 184, 206, 207, 212; mandatory Power for German South-West Africa, 193, 199, 210, 217.
South African Native Affairs Commission, 206.
South African Republic, 145.
South African War, 102, 103.
Spain and Africa, 32, 33, 37, 41, 77, 109, 195.
   Morocco, 104, 106-8.
   North Africa, 25, 64, 110, 120, 121, 192.
   West Africa, 62, 96. *See also* Fernando Po *and* Spanish Guinea.
— political relations with France, 102-4, 107, 108.
Spanish Guinea, or Muni, 102-3, 109, 113, 180, 195.
Speke, Capt. J. H., 68.
'Spheres of Influence', 97, 212-13.
Stanley, Sir H. M., 69-71, 77, 79-83.
Sudan, the, 27, 89, 96, 100, 101, 115, 131, 132, 166, 168, 177, 188, 189, 191, 194, 210.
Sudanese troops, 198.
Suez Canal, 18, 64, 129, 131, 177.
Swaheli, 170.
Swakopmund, 182-5.
Swaziland Protectorate, 143.

Table Bay, 14, 15.
Tabora, 187.
Tajoura, 89, 110.
— Bay, 63, 89.
Tana river, 16.
Tanga, 15, 187.

Tanganyika, Lake, 68-70, 101, 109-12, 114-16, 165, 186.
Tanganyika Territory (formerly German East Africa), 16, 163, 164, 168-70; British mandate for, 210.
Tangier, 27, 32, 105, 108, 113.
Tenures of the Empire, 209-10.
Tewfik, Khedive, 130.
Theal, Dr., 148.
Timbuktu, 65, 66.
Togoland, 88, 96, 111, 152, 153, 161, 176, 197; campaign in, 177-80; French mandate for, 193.
Tordesillas, Treaty of, 37.
Transvaal, the, 113, 142, 146, 147.
Treaty ports, 215.
Tripoli, 19, 65, 96, 176, 192; Italian occupation, 109-10, 127.
Tropical regions, problems of the, 202-5.
Tunis, 23, 89, 119, 123, 192; French Protectorate, 79, 126, 194.
Tunisian troops, 198.
Turkey and Africa, 89, 177.
   East coast, 26.
   Egypt, 18, 19, 100, 127-8, 131-2, 194.
   North Africa, 26, 64, 96, 192.
   Tripoli, 127, 176, 192.
   Tunis, 126.
— war with Italy, 109-10; part in the late campaigns, 189, 191; elimination of interests in Africa, 193-4.
Turkish Capitulations and extra-territorial privileges, 131-2, 213-15.

Ubangi river, 109.
Uganda Protectorate, 98, 102, 164, 165, 167-8.
— railway, 102, 114, 115, 165, 167, 168, 187.
United States and Liberia, 56-7, 194.
Universities Mission to Central Africa, 175.
Upington, 185.
Urundi, Sultanate of, 168, 193.
Usumbara, 169, 186.

Utica, 19.
Utrecht, Treaty of, 43–4, 47.

Vandals, the, 25.
Van Deventer, General, 188.
Versailles, Treaty of, 193, 216.
Victoria, Queen, 103.
Victoria (town), 62, 94, 161, 165.
Victoria Falls, 16, 67, 115.
Victoria Nyanza, 68, 69, 101, 102, 111, 114, 116, 165, 186, 187.

Wadai, 101, 189–91.
Wad Draa (or Nun) river, 108.
Wadi Halfa to Khartoum railway, 114, 115.
Wad Mulaya river, 108.
Walfish Bay, 14, 88, 113, 134, 182, 184.
West Africa, 9, 13, 15, 60, 150–63 ; and the slave-trade, 9, 42–8, 50, 53–6.
West African Frontier Force, 156–7, 178, 179, 181, 182, 198.

West India regiment, 178.
West Indies, 204 ; and the slave-trade, 43, 46, 48, 49, 51, 52.
Whydah, 95.
Wilberforce, William, and the slave-trade, 48.
William II, ex-Kaiser, 105.
Windhoek, 185 ; wireless station, 183.
Wingate, Sir Reginald, 189.
Wireless stations, 179, 183.
Woolf, Leonard, 133, 174.

Yola, 181.

Zambesi river, 14, 16, 18, 27, 67, 92, 93, 110, 112, 114, 115, 134, 164.
— Lower, 67.
— Upper, 67.
Zanzibar, Sultanate of, 15, 68–70, 90–2, 166–7, 210; British Protectorate, 92.
Zulus, 30, 31, 147.

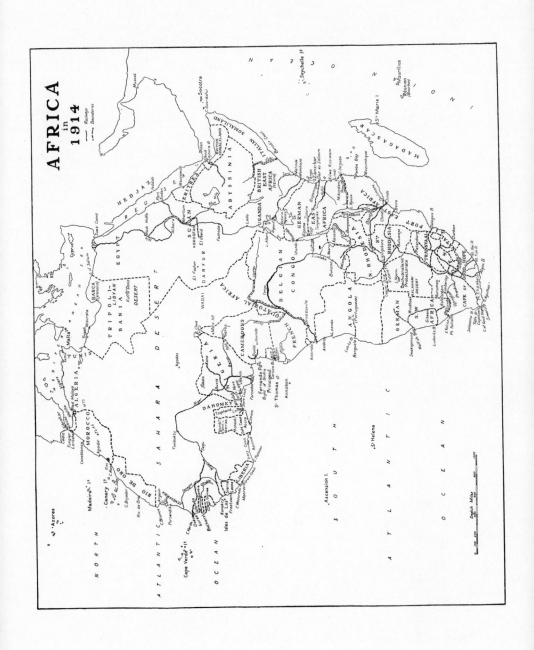

AFRICA
in
1914

Railways
Boundaries